H
EXCELLENCE

Dialogues on Virtue Theory

Daniel A. Putman

University Press of America,® Inc.
Lanham • New York • Oxford

Copyright © 1998
University Press of America,® Inc.
4720 Boston Way
Lanham, Maryland 20706

12 Hid's Copse Rd.
Cummor Hill, Oxford OX2 9JJ

Library of Congress Cataloging-in-Publication Data

Putman, Daniel A.
Human excellence : dialogues on virtue theory / Daniel A. Putman.
p.   cm.
Includes index.
l. Ethics. 2. Virtue. I. Title.
BJ1025.P87 1998   170—dc21   98-23955   CIP

ISBN 0-7618-1161-3 (cloth: alk. ppr.)
ISBN 0-7618-1162-1 (pbk: alk. ppr.)

Contents

Preface

Character is fundamental to ethics. Our actions flow from the kind of person we are and, as Aristotle clearly saw, "kind of person" is defined by the **habits** and **character traits** we develop over a lifetime. The purpose of the following dialogues is to explore the role of character in ethical theory. This approach to ethics, known as **virtue ethics** or **virtue theory**, is becoming an important topic not only in the college classroom but in society at large.

Human Excellence can be used in two ways. First, it could be a basic text in an introductory ethics course. Course sections on relativism, egoism, utilitarianism, and Kant as well as topics like feminist ethics and medical ethics dovetail well with particular dialogues. The dialogues are designed for introductory students who are unfamiliar with philosophy or ethical theory. All ethical positions in the book are thus spelled out in plain language and the book can serve as a foundation for further lecture material. Second, the book could serve as a useful supplement to other ethics texts. *Human Excellence* explains virtue theory in significantly more detail than other books intended for basic ethics courses. Topics like character development, parenting, self-deception, and friendship engage introductory students about fundamental questions in their lives. The book can thus provide instructors with a number of important issues for discussion that are not covered in other texts.

The book is divided into two parts with each part divided into three subsections. The first part is set at a conference on medical ethics and is designed to explain the relationship of virtue theory to other ethical theories. "Thursday" of Part I discusses the origins of virtue ethics, especially in Aristotle, and deals with the challenge of relativism as applied to virtue. "Friday" is about the relationship of virtue to ethical egoism and utilitarianism. "Saturday" deals with virtue and rights theories and the role of virtue in medical ethics. Part II deals with several issues central to virtue theory today. The "awards ceremony" is about honor, self-love and virtue and the importance of parenting for developing good character in children. The "conference on feminism and ethics" deals mainly with the relationship of virtue ethics and feminist theory, especially the "ethics of care." That subsection also touches on a possible relationship of virtue ethics and aesthetics. The last subsection, the "after-dinner discussion," is designed to analyze three topics of special significance to students - courage, self-deception, and the role of friendship in character development. All three are issues that I have found important in the lives of today's college students. Discussion questions related to particular portions of the dialogue follow each subsection.

Acknowledgments

I wish to thank my colleagues in the UW Colleges Philosophy Department for their intellectual support and advice over the years, especially V. Alan White, Roger Rigterink and David Louzecky. Special thanks also to Kathy Hosmer and Bill Bultman without whose practical help this book would not exist.

Part I

Setting: A conference on medical ethics.   Among those attending are four old college friends: Professor Mary Ann Meyer, Professor of Philosophy at the state university, Professor Sharon Rice, Professor of Psychology at the same school, Dr. Elaine Johnson, Head of Internal Medicine at a large local hospital, and Professor James Andrews, Professor of Ethics at a well-known private college in another part of the state. After seeing each other in the hotel lobby, they agree to meet at a local restaurant for dinner and for discussion of "old times." At the restaurant the conversation turns to Professor Meyer's paper on virtue and medicine to be delivered the next day.

Thursday

Johnson: I can tell you my first reaction when I hear the word "virtue." It sounds like something from the 1800's - men were supposed to be gentlemen and ladies were supposed to be virtuous.   I think that usually had something to do with sex, or avoiding sex.   My colleagues might get some good laughs over that.

Meyer: That's a real distortion of what the word means in ethics. All the term meant in Victorian England was following society's narrow code of conduct. Virtue's a lot richer concept than most people think.

Johnson: I remember the word from the couple philosophy classes I took. As I recall Socrates was always arguing that people ought to be virtuous but he could never tell anyone how they were supposed to do that. The whole thing seemed awfully vague to me.

Meyer: I hope I can make the idea clearer for your medical colleagues tomorrow. Virtue has to do with character, with certain habits of living. Aristotle argues that our character traits have a lot to do with the quality of the life we live. Virtues are character traits that promote human growth or human excellence. Examples would be courage, generosity and justice. Vices are traits that have the opposite effect. Someone who's cowardly, for example, will tend not to take risks and will be afraid of new experiences.

Johnson: But what you call "courage" would seem to depend on how each person sees the situation.

Rice: Right. Some people see danger everywhere. Other people get bored easily and love to take risks.

Andrews: That's why Aristotle makes reason an important part of virtue. Courage guided by reason develops excellence by helping a person face the risks and dangers of life. Everybody has to face risks at times but it's not just acting blindly. It's facing dangers intelligently. Aristotle says virtue is acting on a mean relative to us guided by reason. Applying reason is critical.

Rice: That definition doesn't do much for me. What's the "mean"? I don't think he's using the word the same way we do in psychology.

Johnson: And you just said "relative" and that's my point. Whether somebody's a coward or not seems relative to the person. I agree with Sharon. Virtues seem really abstract to me.

Andrews: OK. Let me put it differently. Aristotle is arguing that our character is made up of habits, especially habits of desire. I don't think that's abstract. He's right! We all go through life acting in certain ways based on certain patterns of desire. In different situations in life people with virtuous characters will make the best decisions because their desires are reasonable. But the opposite holds too. Desires can be unreasonable. Some people go crazy with their credit card and buy more than they can afford, for example, or they can't control their temper. I guess I don't see why that's abstract. We see it in our own lives and in people around us all the time.

Johnson: I can accept that people make bad decisions because their desires are unreasonable or out of line. My problem is claiming that courage or having the right amount of anger or whatever is some shared human trait. It's too variable. I still get caught up on the word "relative."

Meyer: Look, isn't it true that sometimes we can overreact and underreact?

Johnson: Sure, I overreact to my teenage son a lot. I guess some parents don't react enough.

Meyer: Well, doesn't the amount of reaction depend on what the situation calls for? In other words, isn't there a "best" level of reacting relative to that situation? Depending on what your son does, sometimes you ought to react at one level, at another time at a different level. And doesn't the best level of reaction also relate to your own personal history? Some people have hot tempers that they have to be careful about.

Johnson: Sure.

Meyer: But then the best response is not "all relative" in the sense that anything goes. The mean or appropriate level is relative to the situation and to your knowledge of yourself but, given those facts, there really are better or worse responses.

Johnson: I'll buy that. My response to my son depends on the situation, how tired I am, if I had a bad day, things like that. I'm always working to find the best response to the situation without going overboard. Some ways to respond are better than other.

Rice: I think part of it might be how mature a person is. Mature people tend to respond better in different situations. There are a lot of 40-year-old immature people running around who act like kids yet. If I understand you, Mary Ann, Aristotle is saying we ought to act reflectively in different situations, not just act blindly.

Meyer: Right. That's close to what he refers to by a mean relative to us and guided by reason. The only difference is that his emphasis is not so much on action as on your inner state or character. Anger's a good example that he talks about. If I get really angry at my own son, sometimes after thinking about it I know that my emotions were out of line. My actions were stupid but I did them **because** my emotions were not well-trained. I might need to work on that. Self-reflection and knowing myself are important. Aristotle would say that I would then be teaching myself to be virtuous about anger. Maybe I can improve my character somewhat by moderating my anger to better fit different situations.

Johnson: So are extremes bad?

Meyer: Aristotle argues that they are. Think of anger again. And remember that what might be too much anger in one situation may be reasonable in another. Like the example with your son - the right level is what is appropriate for the situation. What Aristotle means by "extremes" are unreasonable emotions that have no guidance, no rudder, so to speak.

Rice: Desires that are divorced from reflective thought?

Meyer: Yes. I think psychology can supply many examples of extreme and undisciplined emotions. Child abusers are notorious for having undisciplined anger that goes way beyond what reason calls for. On the other extreme, some people never get angry even when it would be appropriate. They may suppress anger and not be assertive when they should be. In general, unreasonable people tend to have undisciplined emotions. Their actions reflect that and they have a tough time acting appropriately in situations. They're afraid too much or they get too angry or they can't control how much they eat or drink.

Johnson: OK, so Aristotle's talking about reasonable and appropriate desires. But wouldn't that prevent us from acting on new ideas or changing our life in some radical way? I think of the "mean" as average. It sounds like a conservative or boring approach to life.

Meyer: I see your point, but "average" isn't what Aristotle meant. I can give you a good example of what virtue means. I have quite a few older students who are going to college for the first time. A lot of them are tired of jobs in mills or whatever that never challenge them. They want more fulfilling lives. I often tell my classes that those students are virtuous in the Greek sense of the term. They are developing their minds and using untapped potential. In Aristotle's terms their reason has told them that their current state in life is not developing excellence. One woman told me that emotionally she felt really comfortable in her old job but her mind kept telling her she could do more. Great example. It took real courage for her to give up her secure life and go to college. Having your emotions guided by reason does **not** mean being boring. It might really challenge you to do more with life. When you have greater skills and abilities maybe your old desires need to change so you can become a better person.

Rice: I suppose there could be extremes here also. If you're unhappy with your life, you might get depressed or do something thoughtless that actually is harmful to you.

My colleagues in clinical practice see that frequently. In those cases reason doesn't guide desire.

Meyer: Right.

Johnson: I can see the personal development you're talking about, but what's the moral angle in all this?

Meyer: Morality isn't isolated from other parts of life for the Greeks. A person's life is like a tapestry with many parts woven together - your mind, body, desires, relationships. Somebody who habitually lies is simply not going to develop themselves to the fullest. They're going to be suspicious of other people, worry about getting caught, and be victims of their emotions. Knowing our strengths as well as our failures is a major step toward what Aristotle called *eudaimonia* or happiness. He says happiness is living well, not "well" in the sense of a lot of money or goods, but living your life through developing your potential as a human being.

Rice: Sounds like Maslow in psychology. Happiness is self-actualization.

Meyer: They're not the same though. If I remember what people like Maslow are saying, they put less emphasis on reason.

Rice: Yes. Maslow talks about being spontaneous and choosing to be your unique self. He often criticizes what he calls the old concepts of discipline and training.

Meyer: Aristotle wouldn't buy that at all. It's true all of us have unique characteristics and those are important. But for Aristotle we also share a common human essence - our *psyche* or mind - and using reason to guide our life as a member of the human species is critical. The word "fulfillment" for Aristotle means rationally developing your life as much as possible. That doesn't mean suppressing or putting down our desires and emotions but it does mean reflecting on them and guiding them. Those desires then lead to developing the skills, abilities, and relationships we have and include what we would call today living morally.

Rice: I suspect people like Maslow were reacting against a view of reason as a force to keep emotions under wraps - like Freud's superego.

Meyer: Maybe - that's not Aristotle though. Aristotle's no prude. Enjoy the pleasures of life, express your desires - but use your reason to guide those desires. Your actions then will express better who you are as a well-rounded person. That leads to a deeper level of human fulfillment - what he means by happiness. When desires aren't guided by reason, we develop extreme and harmful habits and tendencies. Those are vices.

Johnson: The only other time in my life I heard the word "vice" was in my childhood religion classes. My teachers used to say it was the same thing as sin. This seems a lot different from what I heard in church when I was growing up.

Andrews: It is.

Meyer: Yes. One of the things that really hit me when I first studied the Greeks was how different their view of vice was from that of much of the Judaeo-Christian tradition. I always thought of doing wrong as disobeying God's laws. For Aristotle it's much more a personal failing that's not related to being punished in an afterlife. If you mess up your life, you have harmed yourself.

Andrews: It has more to do with habits than particular actions that are right or wrong or that you get punished for.

Johnson: But actions are what count. I mean, if a physician is
              careless during an operation, someone may die.

Meyer: Sure but habits are critical in whether a doctor or any
              other professional consistently does her job well.
              People make mistakes - everyone does - but someone in
              the habit of working hard whose desires are reasonable
              and who can judge situations well will make far fewer
              mistakes than someone whose life is dominated by
              habits of vice.

Johnson: Habits of vice. Sounds like something from an old
              catechism but I guess Aristotle didn't mean it that way.

Meyer: And isn't the phrase accurate? Don't we develop habits
              in which our desires consistently run us aground?
              What's wrong with calling those habits of vice?
              Someone who can't control her desire to own things
              may destroy her life in bankruptcy. As Aristotle would
              say, such a desire needs the guidance of reason. What
              other term would be better? Some of those negative
              habits may go back many years in a person's life.

Johnson: But a lot of times I know what I should do but don't.
              It's not like the desire is completely unguided by
              reason. I procrastinate a lot. That's a good example. I
              know what's best but keep putting it off and can't get
              myself to do it.

Meyer: Aristotle discusses that also. We do know exactly what
              we should do at times - reason does function - but we
              can't get ourselves to do it. He calls that *akrasia* -
              sometimes translated as weakness of will. True vices
              for Aristotle are deep character traits in which
              unguided desires govern important parts of our lives.
              But people may not be particularly vicious and still
              experience *akrasia*. An example would be eating too
              much at a restaurant when we know it's bad for us. It
              may not be a big habit and we know we shouldn't do it
              but we do it anyway.

Andrews: *Akrasia's* a very common experience.

Johnson: Yes. I know what you mean by the term. We really don't have a good English word for not acting on what we know we should do. So somebody could have *akrasia* without necessarily having a real vice in an area, like eating for example. A person just slips once in a while. But could somebody with a major vice have *akrasia*? It would seem not. A deep habit would be one where you wouldn't think about whether it was good or bad for you. The habit would be too deeply ingrained.

Meyer: They might have *akrasia* in other areas or they might have it a little in the area of the vice. Someone who habitually gets too angry - or maybe the opposite, never expresses anger - still might know in the back of his or her mind what a better level of anger would be and that they ought to act on it.

Rice: Psychologically it would seem that people with vices might be easier to cure once they become aware of the problem. Giving them guidelines would give them a rock or anchor to latch onto.

Johnson: Yes. I see that with people who are addicted to drugs or alcohol and who feel that the hospital staff or people at AA have given them a lifeline.

Meyer: I see your point. That might happen at times but Aristotle would say that's not true of most people. He says that someone with *akrasia* is easier to cure than someone with a habit of vice because the person with *akrasia* at least is thinking about the desires and knows what's best. They have a plan, so to speak. They just need to act on it

Johnson: Maybe. A lot of adults I see in my office have habits of pleasure that really hurt them. Smoking's a good example. Some of them know how bad it is and have tried to quit but can't. They always slip back. I guess that would be a form of *akrasia.*. But many of my patients don't have any intention of doing something better until they end up hitting rock bottom or some crisis. Until that point they just mindlessly keep doing what's bad for them. I don't know who is easier to cure but I can tell you for sure that a spot on the lungs or a heart attack wakes a lot of people up. In our pleasure- oriented society I think some of the worst vices people have are about moderating their level of pleasure.

Meyer: The examples you gave about bad habits of pleasure Aristotle would call intemperance.

Johnson: That's another word we don't hear much - intemperance.

Meyer: What it meant to Aristotle was a deeply ingrained habit of pleasure that was consistently misguided. I had a student once who said she was a love addict - always needed to be physically reassured that she was worth something. That's an example. The addiction to nicotine you mentioned would be another. Aristotle says at one point that intemperate people pursue harmful desires because that's what they are persuaded to do. He says many times that the intemperate person actually decides to do something harmful.

Johnson: I see that a lot. I've seen people take drugs or smoke for all kinds of reasons - peer pressure, rebelliousness, escape from boredom, maybe relief from stress. They harm themselves severely because they somehow think they're doing themselves a favor - maybe showing independence from parents or trying to be part of a group. They never think about the harm they're doing because they convince themselves there's some good in it.

Meyer: I think there are a lot of reasons people don't think about a vice or about the fact that they're developing a bad habit. One is that it's too much work. Desires are sometimes really powerful. It's just easier to let desires dominate our reason rather than the other way around.

Rice: And people often pick up bad habits as children. I have the most sympathy for them. They didn't have much choice, at least at the beginning.

Andrews: Right. If a child develops a destructive habit like lying or an intemperate habit like eating poorly, it's hard to say that the child made any decision to choose that. Aristotle says that children don't have their reason developed enough for them to guide their desires well.

Johnson: I think that's true from what I know of my own children.

Meyer: I'm not sure I completely agree. Children beyond a certain age do make some choices but you're right that most of it is peer pressure or family. And there definitely are cases where children from destructive homes develop some really harmful habits at a very young age. It's not a choice for them at all. I think an adult can pick up vices too and not be conscious of them.

Andrews: Wait, Mary Ann. I agree about the kids, but I'm not so sure about adults. It seems to me that any adult who starts smoking or lying or getting overly angry in situations knows that something is wrong.

Johnson: Sorry, Jim. I'm with Mary Ann on this one. I've seen plenty of adults in my practice who have destructive habits and who started them without much thought or choice. And the habits weren't all picked up as children. Many adults drink too much because of social pressure. Same for smoking. Fear or anxiety or stress just takes control and they never think about it.

Meyer: That's true for things like lying and boasting too. Someone who thinks that being successful in our society means getting ahead at any cost may become boastful because it seems like the right thing to do or they may get in the habit of lying because they think it's necessary. It's not all *akrasia*.

Andrews: I think your patients, Elaine, might be exceptions. I would still argue that most vices for adults begin as weakness of will. I find it hard to believe that an adult can develop a bad habit and not at some point early on know it is harmful.

Johnson: I still don't agree with you. You're giving people a lot of credit for rationality. We develop character traits for lots of reasons. I've seen people that have lost almost all their rational control because of some chemical imbalance or because of some brutal parent. Some of it may even be in our genes. Most bad habits can start and go a long way before the person thinks about changing, if they think about it at all.

Rice: I like some of the points Aristotle makes but overall I think our knowledge now of human biology and psychology shows the old Greek view to be a little simplistic.

Meyer: Yes and no. I was thinking about my fear of heights. That might be a good example of what we mean by emotions simply taking control. I know what that's like. Emotions just overwhelm us at times. In that sense I agree with you. I think our knowledge of the effect of early learning and our increasing information about the brain and genetics is a real advance in self-knowledge over the Greeks. In fact, one of the points I'm going to argue tomorrow is that medicine ought to use its knowledge of the human body and human emotions to talk more about developing human excellence. They argue against smoking all the time. But you rarely see a pediatrician on TV using evidence to talk about the emotions and desires involved in being a parent. I think this is an incredibly important moral issue for today's society.

Rice: So do I. Parents today really need and want more emotional guidance for their own development as parents and the development of their children. I think you're right about us making advances but we don't use that knowledge very often to promote virtue.

Andrews: And I'm not sure *akrasia* is a dead issue either. I know what you mean about emotional ruts being so deep that people may have no control. But I think a lot of times I just plain don't **want** to do what's best, even though I'm fully aware of what I should do.

Johnson: Sure, but I'm never going to tell a patient they're suffering from "weakness of will." It sounds like you're inventing some kind of pseudo-disease. I find it much more useful to talk about conflicting drives.

Andrews: I can see where such language is more useful for physicians but I still think Aristotle had a strong point. It doesn't all come down to chemicals or early learning. Adults do make decisions. I always like the work of art metaphor. You can think of your life as a block of stone and your choice of behavior as the sculpting process; then you can turn your life into a work of art or you can botch it up. If you consistently go for immediate gratification then the life you're forming will reflect that. Habits become ingrained as lifestyles. Desires unmoderated by reason can sometimes actually destroy a person's life and sometimes the people around the person. To say it's a conflict of drives doesn't capture the actual **choice** you make in turning away from something you realize is better.

Rice: Yes, Jim, but people don't start out as uncarved blocks. Parents and other influences sculpt our life long before we have any say about it. Social classes and income levels severely affect the quality of life and the decisions we're able to make. And some of the emotional results of those influences are horrible.

Meyer: Definitely. We realize those effects much more deeply than the Greeks did.

Rice: Then it seems to me that the idea of developing virtue doesn't make sense unless you add in some modern ideas. We all have to work through what we've been given by our upbringing and our society. And all our desires and our decisions are biased to a certain degree by that background.

Andrews: I don't disagree with that. I think all that we're arguing is that as an adult you do have some control over your desires and to that extent you're in control of the kind of life you'll make for yourself. I know it's a weak excuse for me to tell myself that I decided to loaf instead of work because of something in my past. That doesn't hold water. It really is possible to overcome tendencies toward cowardice or greed or dishonesty by using reason to act toward the mean. It's tough at first, but it can be done. I don't think character structures are completely explained by the effect of our environment or experiences we had no control over.

Rice: Well, some of my clinical colleagues might disagree. And speaking of colleagues, I promised to meet one after dinner tonight. I'll have to be leaving but I definitely will be at your talk tomorrow, Mary Ann.

Meyer: Thanks, Sharon. You can cheer me on. Let's get together sometime after the conference is over.

Rice: I'll make a point of it. Take care. Elaine and Jim, good seeing you again. It's been quite a while. Hope to see you around campus sometime.

Johnson: Yes, definitely. Have a safe trip home.

Andrews: Bye, Sharon.

Johnson: Sharon's psychological approach throws a different light on virtue.

Meyer: Yes. It helps bring the theory up to date.

Johnson: But I've been wondering what an anthropologist might say. I took a few undergraduate courses in anthropology. You and I might understand and appreciate the Greek idea of human excellence. But you can't tell me that a tribe like the Yanomamo shares this ideal too. Fierceness and cleverness are their most important character traits. In some cultures downright deceitfulness is prized as a human characteristic. If you're going to make virtue a basis for ethics, how do you handle the fact that cultures differ so much in what they see as the ideal human?

Meyer: That's a question I get a lot in class. Let me toss out another metaphor I find helpful. If you plant an acorn and give it enough water, light and nutrients it will grow into the most fully developed oak tree possible given the original potential in the seed. If some of those features are lacking, the seed may still develop but the tree will be more or less stunted. Aristotle talks this way and gets criticized because of the idea that the tree "tries" to develop to its fullest. Most philosophers and scientists don't like talking about nature that way.

Johnson: With good reason.

Meyer: Yes, but it does make sense to talk about a poor example or a fine example of a species. It's not absurd to say that a dog born with three legs is "abnormal" or that a human child born with a microencephalic brain is "defective."

Johnson: Sure. Medical people use those terms all the time. But what does that have to do with cultural differences?

Meyer: You can think of a culture as supplying the water, light
             and nutrients to a human being. Some cultures
             will supply more and better resources than others.
             Sometimes the physical resources will be limited. A
             society struck by famine will supply such limited
             physical resources to its people that many of them will
             not develop at all. Those children who don't die
             outright will have severe forms of retardation and
             physical deformities because of malnutrition. Our own
             society is by no means exempt here. Growing up with
             violence all around you and always living on the edge
             of fear can make it nearly impossible to have balanced
             and reflective desires in life. Poverty and pollution can
             have devastating effects on human growth. Would you
             say that our society fails in this way to provide an
             environment for full human development?

Johnson: Yes, but I wouldn't blame the famine-stricken society
             you mentioned.

Meyer: Neither would I. The point is that societies can be
             judged as more or less adequate in supplying the
             physical requirements necessary for the development of
             human excellence. Whether they can be blamed for
             that is a different issue.

Johnson: But I still don't see how models of character can be
             compared across cultures.

Meyer: As soon as you admit that societies can be compared in
             how well they meet physical human needs, one of the
             main legs of the cultural relativism argument is
             undercut. Societies **can** be judged. Then the question
             is, does it make sense to say that, beyond physical
             needs, certain psychological and social arrangements
             are better for humans than others?

Johnson: Are you saying the social sciences make claims about
             how humans should live? Some of your colleagues at
             the university might get pretty upset over that. These

are sciences. They study what is, not what should be.

Meyer: That depends on the branch of the discipline they're in. I was talking about this with Sharon on the way down to the conference. Social scientists who emphasize learning as the only way humans become what they are might disagree with me. According to them we are molded by our experiences and culture and the molds are just different, not better or worse.

Andrews: Facts are value-free, including facts about us.

Meyer: Right. That's their view. But a child psychologist such as Piaget and developmental psychologists like Kohlberg and Gilligan would claim that it makes perfectly good sense to talk about better or worse psychological environments in which children can develop their potential. There's nothing absurd in saying that a good environment for a dog is one in which it can run. And I think it makes perfect sense to say that a good environment for young humans is one in which their minds, skills and emotions can be developed most fully. A home with child abuse is a **bad** environment for children. Any society in which child abuse was tolerated would be a bad society for human development. If we admit that societies can be judged and if we admit that some environments are better than others for the physical, psychological, and social well-being of humans, then societies can be judged as more or less virtuous.

Johnson: Sounds elitist. Like we have **the** truth.

Meyer: I know what you mean but think about it a second. We don't consider it elitist to judge a home as bad where parents break their children's arms or make them live in fear through rigid conformity to rules that have no rational basis. Why is it elitist then to judge a society as bad in which the social structures make the inhabitants live in constant fear or in which the highlight of being human is to harm someone else before they get you?

Johnson: But the people **accept** that.

Meyer: But frequently so do family members in an abusive home.   Does acceptance of the structure justify it? Besides, I'm not talking here about going around the world pointing fingers.   The question of whether a society is virtuous or not begins at home.   If elitism means simply having some rationally-based idea of what a fulfilled human life is, then I guess I'm elitist. But if elitism means thinking my own culture embodies that idea then I very much disagree.   I think there are societies around the world that are far more humane in many respects than ours.   Judging other societies is not ethnocentric if you apply the standards equally to yourself and your own society.   And a person had better know a lot about a society before judging it. Just like with individuals, quick judgments are often poorly made.

Johnson: You said you couldn't blame a famine-stricken society for its failure to supply the physical needs of its members.   What about the failure to supply these non-physical needs?   Could you actually blame a society for that?

Meyer: Again a lot would depend on the history and circumstances of the society.   Are you familiar with the Ik, the people discussed in the book *The Mountain People*?

Johnson: I've heard about the book.   Makes for difficult emotional reading I understand.

Meyer: Yes, very much so.   The Ik were forcefully moved by the Kenyan government to make room for a wildlife preserve.   They had been a hunting people for centuries but were moved to the mountains where they were forced to try to scrape out a living in a completely alien environment. The society became terribly destructive with children being thrown out of the home at age three and forming packs that preyed on elderly people. Some of the scenes are incredibly moving. Colin Turnbull, the anthropologist who did the study, became completely disgusted with the Ik. I don't think there's any question that Ik society is very inadequate in developing the potential of its members but I'd hesitate to blame them because of their history and circumstances. It's a different story though for a society that can change but the change doesn't occur because of apathy, greed, or power-seeking on the part of people who control the society. The Ik had no means to change built into their social structures. The whole idea of changing customs is foreign to most subsistence societies. But large modern democracies do have such a means so that a society, for example, that did not move against child or spouse abuse because it was politically expedient not to do so could be held responsible for the human loss it experiences.

Johnson: So you would blame our society for its failings but not the Ik?

Meyer: Right. We have the knowledge, ability and opportunity to change. The Ik didn't. Like we said earlier, certain character traits can be vices but whether or not we blame an individual or a culture for that is a different question.

Johnson: "Blame" talk reminds me of another big problem I have with your virtue idea. This "model human" business has a real dark side. I keep thinking of how what used to be considered "natural" was used against people in the past. People who supposedly weren't "natural," homosexuals, for example, were blamed and persecuted and still are. It seems to me that this is exactly the sort of problem that results from putting the idea of a perfect human into ethics. Why don't we just let people be?

Meyer: It's only a problem if the view of being human is set in
              concrete. I think most modern virtue theorists
              would respond in two ways. First, we've learned a lot
              about human behavior in recent centuries and there's
              no question that great variation exists within the
              concept of human, far more than the ancients realized.
              When the concept of being human got tied to a
              religious or nationalistic idea of the perfect human,
              then the so-called "natural" way became a
              metaphysical club used against people who were
              different than the majority.

Johnson: So you're blaming religion and nationalism and not
              virtue theory?

Meyer: All I'm saying is that certain religious and political
              leaders in history used their idea of the perfect human
              to pressure and at times persecute those who had
              different lifestyles. I'm not blaming all religions and
              governments. Many deeply religious people in history
              deplored and tried to fight this tendency. What I am
              saying is that the problem doesn't lie in having some
              idea of a fully developed person. The problem was that
              this was turned into an absolute idea that was used to
              defend prejudice and hatred.

Johnson: But doesn't the idea of a fully developed person
              automatically lead to some people knowing the "real"
              truth about life?

Meyer: No it doesn't. It should be a matter of evidence, not
              some people having direct pipelines to truth. If we
              don't set the model in concrete, we can revise it as
              evidence indicates. This ties to my second point. The
              concept of human excellence today has its basis in the
              empirical sciences. For example, when a psychologist
              talks about levels of human development, it's subject to
              checking and rechecking and potential modification.

This wasn't the case with the ancients, especially when the concept became tied to a supernatural model.

Johnson: But where do you draw the line between behavior that supposedly supports human fulfillment and the variety of behavior involved in learning? That's an awfully tricky line. People learn to act in a huge number of different ways. How can you judge which ways are better?

Meyer: That's where the scientific and historical information comes in. For example, we've learned that the variety of human sexual relationships is enormous and that many more forms than the "standard model" can be fulfilling. Human sexual desire can express itself in several ways. But we do have some data from history and quite a few studies done in human sexuality. Sexual desire in adults expressing itself toward children, for example, is a twisted and distorted human desire. And, I would argue, having sex with a prostitute as it usually occurs in industrialized societies is a less fulfilling relationship than sex between two partners who care for each other. Someone whose sexual desire could only be focused on uncaring sex objects would represent a type of human tragedy.

Johnson: Wait a minute. There's that strange kind of elitism again. Some people may never have what you would call a fulfilling sexual relationship with a partner who cares about them. Are you telling me that the experiences these people have are somehow inferior?

Meyer: I think there can be many kinds of fulfilling sexual experiences but I don't think that means it's all completely relative. Each person's situation would have to be studied. A lot of so-called normal marriages may have plenty of sexual relations but both partners will tell you they're not very satisfying. Physical and psychological satisfaction are not the same thing. There's a physical level that can be frustrated and there's a psychological level that can be frustrated.

Andrews: I can see what you mean by the physical level. The
             quadriplegic that Richard Dreyfuss played in a movie
             several years ago was a great example of that. I
             think the movie was called *Whose Life Is It Anyway?*
             Dreyfuss did a beautiful job of showing what it would
             be like to have a compelling physical need that could
             not be satisfied. I think that many people in such
             situations really do experience genuine frustration,
             whether it be over the inability to walk or the inability
             to develop a sexual relationship with another person.

Johnson: Yes, but it's the judgment of other people's
             psychological experiences that still bothers me.

Meyer: I don't think it's elitism to say that someone who is
             born without legs or who is born blind is going to miss
             certain very fulfilling human experiences. I'm not
             saying they can't compensate for that and I'm not
             saying they can't in many ways lead **more** fulfilling
             lives overall than people with legs or eyes. But, as is
             well-documented, these individuals themselves
             experience great frustration because they have an idea
             of what it is they're missing.   That's what often
             motivates them to the heroic actions needed to
             compensate for the loss.   Helen Keller is a good
             example.

Johnson: But I want to focus the issue more clearly. Once you
             get beyond physical needs, how can you judge the
             quality of another person's experience? It seems to me
             you're using your concept of a fulfilled human in a way
             that's not justified. You mention marriages in which
             partners find sexual relations unsatisfying. First of all,
             I would not make that judgment about others - people's
             view of what's satisfying is way too diverse.   And
             second, that seems to be a judgment peculiar to modern
             Western thinking.   Whether sex is psychologically
             satisfying is not an issue in most other parts of the

world. I see it as a cultural expectation of ours. It's hardly some sort of universal human need.

Meyer: I'll grant you that, as you talk more about desires and less about actual physical abilities, judgments become more difficult. My own life experience tells me that I should make very few judgments about other people's relationships. But I can still make some. I would still argue my earlier point about the less fulfilling nature of relationships with prostitutes. And a man whose sexual desire involved beating up his spouse or attacking innocent children is someone whose sexual experience is "fulfilling" only in a very perverted way. I don't care what culture he's in.

Andrews: But Elaine's second point is a strong one. It does seem that cultures are the final judge of what is expected. I might grant you the extreme cases like the desires of a child molester but it seems to me that if a culture taught people that relationships with prostitutes were to be expected as highly fulfilling, then they would be. The same holds for expectations within a marriage.

Meyer: I disagree, Jim. Are cultural expectations ends in themselves, the stopping points of all questions about the quality of experiences? Or is it possible that different cultures might light up or hide certain potentialities for humans? I tend to favor the latter.

Johnson: What do you mean by lighting up potentialities?

Meyer: I think it really is an advance to view sexual desire in a psychological as well as physical light. The potential richness is real, not just a cultural invention. Those societies that view sex simply as a physical act, often for the male's pleasure only, are actually leading huge numbers of people to miss out on a much greater richness in the experience. On the other hand, I think our society has lost other high quality experiences, for example, the trust and friendship that were part of the relationship between customers and many small businesses in the 19th century. We've gained efficiency at the cost of losing some significant interpersonal factors in business dealings. Cultural expectations come and go but they don't exist in a vacuum. They light up or hide possible human experiences, some of which might be more fulfilling than others.

Andrews: I still think I'm right that a culture that tells its members to have high expectations will find those expressed in individual expectations. Especially in something as vague as the quality of sexual experiences.

Meyer: To a degree but not completely. I guess I don't think the quality of experiences is completely explained by a culture's expectations. Virtue theory presupposes some common human characteristics and the fulfillment of those characteristics affects the quality of a person's life. The Greeks felt development of the mind and the moderation of desire by reason were very important. I would agree but add more factors involving emotions and human relationships based on work in developmental psychology.

Andrews: Well, I must say I'm looking forward to your paper tomorrow.

Johnson: So am I, though I fear some of my colleagues may view it as a study in antiques.

Andrews: I vote we continue this discussion tomorrow night. I'm sympathetic with virtue theory in many ways, but it seems to me that the other traditional views in ethics have some real strengths that virtue theory lacks.

Meyer: I'd like to meet again. I probably will be more relaxed when the presentation is over. See you tomorrow.

Discussion Questions

1. pp. 2-3: Is Aristotle right that unreasonable desires are the source of many of our problems?

2. p. 4: Aristotle argues that the "mean" applies to many situations in life. Is he right? What might be another example?

3. pp. 4-5: Are undisciplined or unreasonable emotions **ever** good in human life?

4. p. 5: Is "pursuing excellence" what these older students are doing? Or is there another way of looking at this?

5. pp. 6-7: Is Aristotle right that happiness is fulfillment as a human being? How does that relate to what our society says happiness is?

6. pp. 8-9: **Why** do we not do what we know we should do? In other words, why does *akrasia* happen?

7. pp. 9-10: Which is easier to "cure," *akrasia* or a real vice?

8. p. 10: Do most people choose destructive habits because they think the habits are good for them in some way? Or is that an excuse for avoiding responsibility?

9. pp. 11-12: How common is it for a vice to begin as *akrasia*? What might be examples?

10. p. 12: Does TV promote harmful habits? Should TV be used deliberately to promote habits like justice and empathy? Or should such ethical concerns not even be an issue for television?

11. p. 14: Is a person's upbringing ever a genuine excuse for behavior as an adult?

12. pp. 15-16: Is the "growth" metaphor for culture a good one?

13. p. 17:   Can cultures be judged based on their psychological and social environments?

14. pp. 17-18: Is the comparison of an abusive home and a "bad" culture a good one?

15. p. 18:   Does accepting a culture's structure justify that structure?

16. pp. 18-19: Can our society be blamed for its loss of human potential?

17. p. 21:   Is prostitution a less fulfilling human relationship than sex between partners who care about each other? Why or why not?

18. pp. 22-23: Can an outsider judge the quality of another person's experience?

19. p. 23:   Is Andrews right that what people expect out of life is simply what a culture teaches them to expect?

20. pp. 23-24: Is viewing sex in psychological terms an "advance" compared to viewing sex as simply a physical act?

21. pp. 23-24: Has our culture lost other fulfilling human experiences besides the one mentioned?

Friday

Mary Ann Meyer, Jim Andrews, Elaine Johnson

Johnson: I found the response to your talk interesting.

Meyer: Yes, I didn't expect the variety of questions that I got. Medical ethics draws a lot of interest these days.

Andrews: A couple of the questions showed a good background in the issues. I thought the one about "whose virtue are you talking about" was sharp. Don't virtue theorists themselves disagree about what virtues count the most? Not sure you answered that very fully.

Meyer: Well, I do concede that there are variations within virtue theory but I guess I'd point out too that all virtue theorists have some things in common. I probably should have spelled that out better to the questioner.

Johnson: Concern with character?

Meyer: Right, that's one. All virtue theorists emphasize character traits over specific actions or ethical rules. People with a certain character will tend to act in certain ways. And they all agree that virtues have to do with human fulfillment. They sometimes disagree with Aristotle and with each other about which virtues are most significant and whether some traits are or are not virtues.

Andrews: Personally, I've always had trouble with Aristotle's virtue of "magnificence." Powerful and wealthy citizens in Athens were supposed to cultivate this desire to give money or other benefits to the city in a big way. I guess today the leaders in the *Forbes Magazine* list of wealthiest individuals would be the people he'd be referring to. My problem is I don't think that's any different than generosity which Aristotle thinks is a separate virtue. If a poor student acts on the desire to share his limited money, I don't see how that's different from a millionaire who shares his money. Different results maybe and different amounts but same desire.

Meyer: I think I probably agree but I had a student once who claimed that magnificence was a much more complex character trait than generosity. A wealthy person has to cultivate a desire not just to share money but has to cultivate the proper understanding of how to do it well.

Andrews: So how is that different from generosity? If I'm giving ten dollars to a cause, don't I want to apply reason to do it well? It's just on a smaller scale than the millionaire.

Meyer: I'll concede your point though I bet Aristotle might have more to say to you about it. Even though we might have a problem with magnificence, virtue theorists don't have a problem with temperance or courage. That's another point of agreement. Certain virtues are on all the lists. They might give them different names but all would agree that reasonable patterns of pleasure in a person's life or training our desires to face up to difficulties in life are important parts of human growth and development

Andrews: But they sure categorize them differently.

Meyer: Sure. One theorist - Pincoffs - divides virtues into instrumental or useful virtues and noninstrumental virtues.   Courage would be instrumental whereas something like cheerfulness would be noninstrumental. He then subdivides them   further   to   include categories like mandatory and nonmandatory. I'm not sure I always   agree   with   him. He counts sensitivity,   for example, as noninstrumental and nonmandatory. But sensitivity can be very useful in many interpersonal situations and, based on what we know from psychology, may be necessary for a successful relationship like a marriage. I like his analysis in many ways but disagree about certain specifics. But I don't think the fact that we disagree is some sort of critical blow to virtue theory. Like in any other discipline, discussion refines how we think about concepts. It happens in the sciences and humanities all the time. Same in virtue theory.

Andrews: But how can you tell if a virtue should be on the list or not? I guess I don't think of cheerfulness as a virtue at all. It's a nice feature to have but is it important to human fulfillment? I have the same problem with Aristotle's claim that wit or a sense of humor is a virtue.

Meyer: I think the best way of answering the question of what traits are virtues is to go back to the source - human experience. Is a sense of humor important or not? In one way, no. It's a nice addition to life but it doesn't quite rate with courage or temperance. Lack of a sense of humor is nothing like being a coward. But maybe Aristotle had a point. A sense of humor may have something to do with a good outlook on life, especially if you can laugh at yourself at times. And it can put other people at ease.

Johnson: Yes. My patients who can laugh at their own mistakes can forgive themselves and other people. We're all in the same human boat, so to speak.

Meyer: Right, so maybe it is a real virtue. It puts life in perspective. Like I mentioned before, I don't think more than one approach to virtue theory is a major flaw. What virtues should be included is a matter of discussion and checking out what we learn about people. Maybe there are studies about the importance of a sense of humor for psychological stability. I don't know if there are, but such studies would tell us whether a trait like that is important. The key thing is that we keep our minds open to different sources of information and keep the conversation going. A variety of approaches might help us understand better what human happiness is about.

Andrews: I see your point. But one other issue raised this morning really got me thinking. Several people I talked to between sessions mentioned the concern about legal issues in medicine now. I'm not convinced all this increased concern about medical ethics is because of a greater interest in ethics so much as a greater interest in avoiding malpractice suits. I'm a bit of a cynic about people's motivations. These days it pays in cash to know about things like rights and proper conduct.

Johnson: I suspect that angle was in the back of a lot of people's minds this morning. It's hard to be a physician these days and not be concerned about it.

Meyer: You might be right. But no matter why people are more interested in medical ethics, I applaud the results. Your cynical side, Jim, sounds a little like that questioner who asked me if virtue isn't just disguised egoism.

Andrews: I suppose so. I'm not sure that question was completely off-base. Virtue ethics seems on the surface anyway just a refined form of doing what you want to do for yourself. What you said yesterday evening and then today in your talk makes virtue sound like a noble theory but isn't it just a glorified way of being self-centered? Everything is "my character, my development." I sometimes think the Greek philosophers were arguing for egoism.

Meyer: I think there are some big differences between virtue theory and egoism. Egoism says you ought to maximize benefits for yourself as much as possible. The Greek philosophers were trying in their own time to distinguish the self-centered egoism they saw around them from something greater that transcends the individual.

Andrews: How?

Meyer: To live by courage, justice, loyalty and the other virtues isn't just a matter of self-interest; the virtues are the only consistent way to live fully as a human being. A person may not want to work hard, to act justly, to care about others; the person's actual desires may be directly opposed to doing those actions. But when people realize that desires need to be focussed on a higher goal, that realization can pull a person out of his or her egoistic needs.

Johnson: But I know lots of egoists who work for others.

Andrews: Yes. Why couldn't an egoist just say, "OK, I won't do what I want to do right now because in the long run it will pay for me to work hard or care about my neighbor. Delayed gratification is better anyway."

Meyer: An egoist could say that but that's not the focus of the virtues. That's my point. Look, Jim, why after all are we teachers? Let's use our job as an example. After a person goes through all the old jokes about not being in it for wealth, fame and power, the question is a darn good one. And I know one reason I'm in it is that I have an idea of what an educated human being should be and what that means for the quality of

human life. My belief in the potential of my
students is tied to training my desires to do a good
job - even when I don't feel like it. In other words,
being virtuous is tied to the ideals of teaching. I
find teaching fulfilling and I guess I want to make an
impact. But I don't think the only reason for being
virtuous in teaching is my self-enhancement nor is
self-enhancement even a major factor, at least in my
better moments in the classroom. I think the focus on
a higher or finer goal is true of anyone who takes a
project seriously. If virtuous habits are developed and
desires are guided by reason, they put checks on
pure self-interest.

Andrews: I'm tempted to say that teaching's a hidden attempt on
your part to be immortal. My cynical side again. I
guess most of what people do, especially big decisions
like careers, are a combination of motives and goals.

Meyer: Yes, I'm not sure there's such a thing as a completely
pure act or pure motive.

Andrews: I suppose that might lead to an even deeper argument
against egoism. I think Aristotle and virtue ethics in
general have a different view of "self" than egoism
does. Egoism assumes an isolated ego as the starting
point but I think Aristotle doesn't think there is such a
thing.

Meyer: The self is always connected to the world around it.

Andrews: Right. So when Aristotle says we should be virtuous
he assumes there will be a radiating effect on those
individuals around the person. Probably a good
example is his discussion of friendship. The ability to
make deep friends is a virtue because we are naturally
social beings. Caring about others - be it children or
loved ones - is as much a part of who we are as the
need for food, clothing or shelter.

Johnson: Sure, but again, caring about others or having friends could be done for egoistic reasons. I know people like that.

Meyer: So do I. But should we care about our friends or our children mainly for our own benefit? Is that the best way to live a human life?

Johnson: Maybe we don't have a choice. I have a friend who says humans are always naturally self-centered. We always act for own benefit first and foremost whether we realize it or not.

Meyer: That's a little bit different. That's called "psychological egoism" in ethics - everybody is always self-centered all the time.

Andrews: Yes, psychological egoism is a strange theory. If I save a friend from drowning and put my own life at risk, somehow I'm doing it primarily for myself. That's hard to buy. I'll admit I have some interest in doing everything I do; otherwise I wouldn't do it. But that doesn't mean my ego is the **main** goal or focus of the act. The goal and focus is my friend.

Meyer: I don't think many philosophers take psychological egoism very seriously. There are too many strong examples against it and psychological egoists have to twist motives and goals around too much. When they're trying to explain heroic actions, they always have to assume hidden, unconscious motives that are vague and don't seem to fit our experience. I think it's really possible to put other people first at times. A bigger problem for virtue theory is ethical egoism. Ethical egoism says you **should** be out for yourself first. You really can care about others but you shouldn't do that. That's the theory Jim suggested looked like virtue theory. Be courageous, be temperate - it's good for the ego.

Andrews: And what I realized during our discussion a while ago is that the "self" is different in ethical egoism and virtue theory.

Johnson: Excuse this nonphilosopher but what are you talking about?

Meyer: Think about what people mean by "self." Ethical egoism says you should be out for your "self" as much as possible. Consider friendship again. When Aristotle says friendship is a virtue, he means it is good for you - but not just you as some isolated entity. The virtue naturally benefits you **and** others because the "self" is naturally a socially connected entity. There is no big gap between your ego and the rest of the world.

Johnson: So egoism as we mean it is a kind of modern invention?

Meyer: Well, there were real egoistic philosophers in the ancient world too but what Jim and I are saying is that the egoistic view of the self - ancient or modern - is a distortion. Ethical egoists have to shoehorn experiences like friendship into something that should always be for yourself.

Andrews: And that distorts what the experience of friendship is about.

Meyer: Exactly. Aristotle has another virtue that's a good example of this point. It's called truthfulness or honest self-presentation. The extremes are boasting or a false image of superiority on one side and on the other side putting yourself down irrationally, a kind of false humility. An egoist might say, "It doesn't pay for me to be a hypocrite or boaster. People won't trust me and I won't benefit as much in the long run." But that's not the point in virtue ethics. A truthful person will both benefit themselves and benefit others with whom they deal. They will admit mistakes as well as strong points and be able to judge when the claims of others should come first. It's an objective judgment of yourself and the situation and acting accordingly. That's not egoism.

Andrews: That's what I meant about egoism's twisted view of the self. It distorts the reality of our experiences.

Meyer: Right. If the self is naturally a social entity, then naturally a generous person will both benefit self **and** others, a courageous person will learn to overcome fears **and** benefit society as a whole and a truthful person will be able to recognize when her own needs should **not** come first. If her friend or children need her help, a virtuous person will be able to recognize the truth of the situation and not be all wrapped up in her own desires.

Johnson: Egoism is a sort of pathology from this angle.

Meyer: I think it is. It puts out a false view of the "self" and then says you ought to always act with that distorted view of the ego as your goal. It's actually a program for turning your desires into patterns of vice. We are always in relationships of one sort or another.

Andrews: Probably the virtues involving other people show that the best. Being generous or courageous helps other people yet these virtues also fulfill the person doing the action.

Meyer: I think that's also true of a virtue like temperance. An egoist might say about temperance, "Great idea. Eat and drink moderately to avoid health problems. Have sex intelligently to avoid AIDS." That sort of thing. But for Aristotle temperance had to do with what is appropriate in the situation - the mean. The major concern is not avoiding hangovers or STD's.

Johnson: Less concern about consequences?

Meyer: More of an emphasis on what fits the situation. Students in sexual relationships know this well. It's not egoism that makes a successful relationship but an awareness of the other person's needs as well as one's own. Desires that fit the overall situation - temperance - are often the difference between what we call love and what amounts to exploitation. Again, virtue theory assumes a self that's always in relationship to the surrounding world.

Johnson: Ah, here comes Dave. I told him we'd be meeting here. Mary Ann and Jim, I'd like you to meet Dave O'Brien. Dave's another internist at the hospital and he's on the hospital's ethics committee. Dave, this is Mary Ann Meyer and Jim Andrews. I think you're familiar with Mary Ann from her talk earlier today. Jim's a philosopher also and interested in medical ethics.

O'Brien: Pleasure to meet you. When Elaine mentioned your conversation last night and said that you were going to continue it tonight, I asked if I could sit in. She said she didn't think you'd mind.

Meyer: You're very welcome to join us. Philosophical conversations are never closed sessions.

Andrews: Yes, welcome. We've just been hashing over the differences between virtue theory and egoism. Mary Ann's been arguing that virtues involve a different view of the self from egoism.

O'Brien: In what way?

Meyer: Basically, virtue theory assumes that we are always in relationship with the world around us. Virtues, especially virtues directed toward other people, maximize happiness both for the person and others.

O'Brien: That idea of maximizing happiness I've seen before. In my work on this ethics committee I've been reading quite a few philosophers. A lot of them talk about intrinsic goods, higher goods, etc. As I recall, the utilitarians make the "greater good" a cornerstone of their theory. I know you talked this morning about developing human potential. How is that different from the utilitarians?

Meyer: You have to consider where the utilitarians are coming from. Utilitarianism is concerned with the consequences of actions. They argue that consequences are what really count in ethics. When the utilitarians talk about maximizing happiness they mean producing the greatest amount of good possible in a situation for the greatest number of people. A simple example would be if you had $100 to give away and had a choice between equally helping 50 people in one option and 25 people in the other, who should you give the money to? The 50.

O'Brien: That's like many of the examples we run into in medical ethics. Should we spend limited resources on new expensive technologies or on programs promoting wellness or on increasing staff so patients get more personal attention? It's a debate about priorities.

Meyer: Right and you want to do the actions that produce the best all-round amount of good for the most people. That's classic utilitarianism.

Johnson: But what's this "good" they're talking about? I guess I'd raise some of the same skeptical points I raised yesterday. Isn't that all pretty vague?

Andrews: The utilitarians base their idea of good on what people enjoy - what has an intrinsic value to people - pleasure, for example. Jeremy Bentham, who first really developed utilitarianism around 1800, thought pleasure was the most basic intrinsic value.

Johnson: So does a sadist.   Does a sadist's pleasure count?   I
            hope not.

Andrews: Good point.

Meyer: Yes, that seems to throw a wrench into pleasure being
            the standard.   If you weigh the pleasure of a sadist
            versus the suffering of a victim, which is more
            important? The whole idea sounds crazy.

O'Brien: So then what?

Meyer: A lot of utilitarians object to pleasure.   John Stuart
            Mill did and suggested happiness instead. Mill says at
            one point that he would rather be Socrates dissatisfied
            than a pig satisfied. He's implying there's a lot more to
            human happiness than pleasures. The problem is that
            "happiness" also seemed vague to a lot of utilitarians
            so today many simply say the fulfillment of desires is
            the basic good.

Johnson: But doesn't that leave the same problem that pleasure
            does? I can think of some pleasures that I would not
            call good and I can think of some desires that
            would best be left unfulfilled.

Meyer: That's exactly where I think virtue theory enters the
            picture. I see virtue theory as complementary to the
            other major theories in ethics. I don't think they are
            rivals. The fact that we don't want to call all pleasures
            or all desires good shows that we have some concept of
            human fulfillment in mind that we can use to judge
            pleasures and desires. I mean, what makes some
            desires "bad?" I think some concept of human nature
            and human fulfillment is implied in their theory.

O'Brien: But don't utilitarians argue that all desires are equal if
            the greatest number served is the same? If I remember

my reading, the important thing is greatest good for greatest number, not what **kind** of desire it is. If the greatest number served in a situation happens to be one - myself - then that certainly seems right. How can you judge pleasure or desires when you yourself are the only one involved?

Johnson: Elitism again, Mary Ann?

Meyer: I don't think so. The utilitarians were arguing against some irrational views of desire in their time and to a great extent I think they were right. Many desires that were judged in the past to be harmful to human beings are not so.

Andrews: I just ran into a great example to support the utilitarian point. I found an 1895 edition of *The People's Common Sense Medical Advisor* in a used bookstore. A certain Dr. Pierce spends over fifteen pages explaining how masturbation leads to insanity and to a disease called "spermatorrhea" which is supposed to cause just about everything bad.

O'Brien: Medicine has such a long and honorable history!

Andrews: So does philosophy! The view of women taken by many philosophers in the past is a matter of great embarrassment now. This is exactly the sort of thing the utilitarians were fighting - judgments about the qualities of human beings that were nothing but prejudices in disguise.

Meyer: I agree completely. But the question remains: does that mean that we have no rational standards at all by which to judge desires in themselves? Let's take the situation Dave mentioned where only one person is involved. Person A is a necrophiliac. Assume that he expresses his desires in ways that do not disturb the desires of anybody else. Person B enjoys listening to classical music, a very personal and intense experience

for him.   Is it an irrational prejudice in favor of
classical music that makes me think that necrophilia is
a pleasure showing a human defect while that is not
true of enjoying music? I don't think so. I think there
are good grounds in studies of human development
that permit us to judge desires in themselves.

Johnson: Would that go for interpersonal acts too?

Meyer: Sure. The utilitarians are right that child molesting is
wrong because of the terrible consequences to the
victim. But it seems to me they never go far enough.
Why exactly are those consequences bad? It's because
of what the act will do to the child's future
development as a human being. Utilitarians usually
stop at the point of saying that, other factors being
equal, frustrating desires is bad. But that's not enough.
Some desires should be frustrated - an alcoholic's
desire for a drink, for example. It's not the frustrating
of desires that makes an act bad. It's the prevention of
fulfillment as a human being.

O'Brien: But adults vary enormously in what the word "growth"
would mean.

Meyer: And that's one of the strong utilitarian points.   We
have to be extremely cautious in judging other people's
desires. Benefit of the doubt should always go to
the other person who has a different background and
different interests than us.   But we still can make
judgments with good reasons in certain cases. Raising
a spoiled child is not good for the child because,
without self-discipline, her desires will not be guided
by reason and she will have trouble making difficult
decisions as an adult.   She'll probably develop
destructive habits.   An alcoholic whose family life is
being destroyed has his desires skewed when he places
a desire for a drink over developing love and justice for
the people around him. It's possible to judge between
desires based on the effect of the desire on the

individual's development as a human being.

Andrews: But you **are** talking consequences.

Meyer: Sure but the standard for judging those consequences has to do with a concept of what it is to be human. Virtue ethics focusses on character and human nature. Utilitarianism focusses on consequences of actions. But those actions flow from certain character traits and the results are judged by some standard of human fulfillment.   I think the two theories are complementary.

Johnson: Maybe, but I still think the utilitarians are a lot more down to earth. You point out that they have problems but the issue gets even more confusing when you try to make vague distinctions about kinds of pleasures and degrees of human fulfillment.

Meyer: This is probably the biggest challenge to contemporary virtue theory. If the theory is going to hold up over time, it's going to have to be applicable to real life. And to do that means it's going to have to be more precise about what human "fulfillment" means and what that has to do with ethics.

Andrews: I think MacIntyre may have taken a step in the right direction.

Meyer: Yes.

O'Brien: Are you talking about *After Virtue*?   I've seen it referred to in several of the things I've been reading.

Andrews: Yes. MacIntyre spells out in some detail what "virtue" has meant in Western history. And he himself makes some helpful distinctions. For example, he distinguishes between the internal and external goods of practices. If you take most organized human activities, medicine, for example, there are certain rewards that are internal to the practice of that activity and some that are external.

Meyer: That relates to what I said today in my talk when I mentioned that practicing medicine has certain internal goods for the person doing it. Like the sense of satisfaction of giving someone his or her life back or the rewards of doing research on a significant problem.

Andrews: MacIntyre talks about playing chess. The thrill of the competition, the stretching of the mind required to win, the aesthetic quality of the game itself - these are the internal goods. There might also be external goods like money or status in the local or world chess community. Virtues are those traits that are necessary in order to experience the internal goods of practices like chess. Being dishonest may bring a lot of money but the more dishonest a person is in a practice, the less he or she will experience the internal rewards of that practice.

O'Brien: The public doesn't seem to recognize that distinction much. Doctors are always being accused of acting for external rewards like money and status.

Johnson: I'm afraid it's sometimes true but it's much less true than the public thinks. Most of my colleagues are dedicated to their careers.

Meyer: I think the cynicism by the public is a recognition of the difference between external and internal goods. They realize what it means to be personally dedicated to a practice like medicine and they know the effect of big external rewards on that dedication. The large salaries of physicians and their high status cause resentment and confuse much of the public about your real motives. If they think you are in it for the money or status, they won't expect you to act virtuously.

Andrews: MacIntyre says that external goods can corrupt the integrity of a practice in a society and we may be seeing that now to a degree in medicine. We certainly see it in big-time sports.

O'Brien: I can see the distinction you're drawing but I'm not sure what it has to do with ethics exactly.

Meyer: It helps to keep in mind again that both Aristotle and modern virtue theorists tend to see human life holistically - as one interwoven fabric. Corruption of a practice has a great deal to do with what we usually call moral issues - things like cheating, lying, causing suffering. Many people sense there's something wrong with collegiate athletics, to use Jim's example. You get a lot of talk in newspapers about playing basketball or football for its own sake instead of playing it for money. But MacIntyre's analysis is much more fine-tuned. What **are** the internal goods of sports compared to the external ones? Why are college students engaged in sports? Why **should** they be? If students are taught that external rewards are all that count - the money or status - what are we teaching them about life?

Johnson: I'm still not clear what you mean by external goods corrupting a practice. I know some physicians that are in it primarily for the money and status and they're very good at their job **because** of that.

Meyer: That's true of some people but it would be interesting to put those same people in a situation where they could gain financially if they were to practice medicine badly. That would be the real test of why they do what they do. A big reason external goods corrupt is because the focus of the person is on something other than the practice itself. It's on the money, not the practice. The more the focus is on money and status, the more the physicians you mention would be willing to distort or twist the actual practice in order to gain those rewards. It just so happens that good practice leads to money and status but that's an accidental connection. If they're really in it for the money, it could happen at different times that deliberately shoddy practice may be necessary. Maybe an example might be to set up treatment to have a wealthy elderly patient continually coming back for help when he or she doesn't need it. So much for trust in the doctor-patient relationship! It would certainly corrupt the practice for that patient.

O'Brien: There seems to be a larger social issue also. It's not just the trust of this particular patient but the trust of society in the profession.

Meyer: Exactly. In big-time college sports everyone knows the importance of money and professional contracts for many of the athletes and the programs they're in. I'm not saying collegiate sports can't build character or well-rounded people, but the external rewards are becoming incredibly important and we see constant examples in the paper of what that can do to players and school athletic programs. In the same way, if external rewards were really the sole goal of physicians, how much trust would anyone put in the practice of medicine? Very little because it would always depend on the financial condition of the doctor at the time. External rewards corrupt the long-term stability of practices because mutual social expectations are lost. Trust is destroyed.

Andrews: You know, Mary Ann, it still sounds like utilitarianism. Be virtuous because it has good consequences for most people.

Meyer: But **why** is it bad to have trust destroyed? Because the majority of people simply don't like it? Or is it because it's impossible to develop any kind of human excellence in a society where trust is consistently broken? I'd still argue that if you push utilitarianism you end up with the importance of character and the need for some concept of human fulfillment.

O'Brien: Don't the utilitarians themselves talk about different kinds of goods?

Meyer: Mill talks about higher and lower pleasures and says that people who experience both will give a strong preference to those that use their higher faculties like their mind.   Mill seems to be implying that some pleasures are more innately fulfilling to human beings.

O'Brien: From my reading of the utilitarians they don't seem to make distinctions much in practice between different kinds of goods.

Meyer: Right. MacIntyre points out that the utilitarians lump goods together. He specifically says that utilitarians can't distinguish between goods internal and goods external to a practice. They sum together the total good of an action.

Johnson: All this talk about internal goods sounds like the old saying, "Virtue is its own reward." I never bought that. I've seen too many good people get stepped on.

Meyer: I do buy it.   I think the rewards that really count require virtue. For one thing, if you are ever going to get competent at something, you have to act virtuously in doing it. The person who cheats consistently will never learn how to play a game well. Good data from psychology indicates that competence is an inherently strong motivator in humans. It's extremely satisfying in itself.

O'Brien: But I've done plenty of things for external reasons that I've learned to do well.

Johnson: Yes, Mary Ann, that really sounds incredibly idealistic.

Meyer: I'm not denying that someone can become competent for external reasons.   It's like the physicians you mentioned earlier - some are in it for the money or status and do the job well because of that.   All I'm saying is that one reward internal to a practice like medicine is the enjoyment a person gets from being competent in it - being good at it.   The pride of meeting challenges, so to speak.   And certain virtues - honesty, self-discipline, a certain amount of courage - are necessary to achieve that.

Johnson: But what makes this pleasure higher? I can accept that competence requires certain virtues but I'm not sure how the pleasure of competence rates higher than the pleasure of money or status.   Sounds like a philosopher's bias.

Meyer: I don't think so.   There's some fascinating data from psychology again that indicates that people actually prefer competence motivation to external rewards. When external motivations like money are added to situations, enjoyment of the practice at hand actually decreases. It appears to be the case that, other factors being equal, people will take an internal good over an external one.   That's one reason why I'd rate such pleasures higher in Mill's sense - studies indicate that we find them more fulfilling.

Johnson: But other factors are never equal.

Meyer: I don't see how that's a criticism.   The point about favoring internal goods still holds.   My experience is that people who have a job they do mainly for the money will use that money as much as possible to promote a practice they do enjoy.   I think it's those kinds of practices - those done for enjoyment or a sense of fulfillment - that give people the greatest sense of significance in their lives.   And in those practices virtues are much more important.

O'Brien: I   still   don't   see   how   doing   something   for external reasons involves vice.

Meyer: It doesn't necessarily. But it opens the door to it. I remember several years ago on television they interviewed a worker in a large automobile plant in Detroit. His job was to use a lift of some sort to carry auto bodies from one side of a warehouse to the other. He couldn't care less about the job, was in it for the money, and in order to make his job more interesting he would periodically drop one of the auto bodies. It didn't bother him. External goods redirect our attention. Internal goods integrate us. I think we all know how easy it is to let dishonesty or laziness enter into something we have to do but don't care about doing.

O'Brien: Your point about lack of job interest reminds me of a friend who's a lawyer. He says he's in it for the money and that shows pretty much in his attitude toward his job. But he has a model railroad collection that's one of the best in the city. The care and time he puts into that would make him the best lawyer in the city if he applied it to his job.

Meyer: And I'll bet he wouldn't cheat when it comes to the integrity of his hobby.

O'Brien: Right. He studies the history of railroads and knows more details about railroads than a hundred other people combined. He's extremely careful in everything he does that's related to his collection. I think his identity is tied up more with his expertise in his hobby than with his job.

Meyer: That's a good example of what we were discussing earlier. Your friend's hard work, conscientiousness and personal honesty when it comes to his hobby are necessary virtues for the enjoyment he gets out of it. He apparently doesn't get that out of his job which he's doing for external reasons. I suspect for other people with meaningless jobs the internal goods might come from family, home, a cottage, or other hobbies. In any case, virtues are necessary in whatever practice people want to be competent.

Andrews: That would also explain the strange view that many people have that a person should be moral at home but not in the business world. Business is supposed to be all external rewards - mostly profit. So why be virtuous unless it looks good for profit?   Home's different.   At home virtue is important because otherwise we couldn't get those internal goods that really count - the things we enjoy most about a close family life.

Meyer: Yes. I think Marx had a strong point that the capitalist business world produces huge amounts of labor divorced from personal integrity. Vices come more easily when the bottom line is profit. The assembly line sure doesn't promote virtue.

O'Brien: That may be changing. I think a lot of businesses now are working to give   their   employees   a   bigger personal share in what happens. And more and more businesses are employee-owned now. I wonder if the level of virtue goes up then.

Meyer: My guess is that it does. I've read some studies that show morale in such businesses is much higher. With more internal goods at stake the level of virtue would rise. But we'll never get away from the pressures of external goods. I think the nature of survival forces that on us. Probably the best we can do is minimize such situations.

Andrews: Utilitarians can still claim the best way of looking at this. I mean, if too much emphasis on external goods corrupts a practice too much - a business, game, whatever - then the practice will be destroyed.   So fewer people will be able to enjoy it. If you're right that internal goods promote the practice, then I'd argue that the internal rewards are better from a utilitarian standpoint. Greater good for greater number.

O'Brien: Like you said, Mary Ann, it seems like the two theories
            need each other. They're not competitive. Anyway,
            there are several points I'd still like to discuss but I'm
            afraid I must leave. My work on the ethics committee
            takes a completely different approach than virtue
            theory. We talk a lot about rights of patients. I'd like
            to get into the differences and similarities between
            rights and virtue theory. Is there any chance we could
            meet one more time?

Johnson: I have to be out of town most of tomorrow so I'll have
            to bow out.

Andrews: My plane connections are for mid-afternoon so I could
            make lunch.

Meyer: I'll be around till 2:00 or so. Would you want to chat
            over lunch here at noon?

Andrews: Sure.

O'Brien: Sounds good. Elaine, I'll see you at the hospital in a
            couple days, I'm sure. Until tomorrow then, Mary Ann
            and Jim. Good night.

Discussion Questions

1. pp. 27-28: Is "magnificence" a different virtue than generosity? Is it a virtue at all?

2. p. 29: Is sensitivity a necessary virtue for human fulfillment?

3. p. 29: Is cheerfulness a virtue?

4. pp. 29-30: Is Aristotle right that "wit" is a virtue?

5. pp. 30-31: Is virtue theory a form of egoism? Or do virtues put checks on egoism?

6. pp. 31-32: Why do you want a career? Why are you in college? Would you call the reason egoistic? Or is it more than that?

7. p. 33: Is psychological egoism an accurate view of human life?

8. pp. 33-35: Does ethical egoism have a faulty assumption about the self?

9. p. 35: What does "temperance" mean to you? Is it more than intelligent egoism?

10. pp. 37-38: Is pleasure our most basic intrinsic value?

11. p. 38: Are there some desires which, aside from bad utilitarian consequences, should best be left unfulfilled? Why?

12. pp. 38-39: Are all desires equal if the greatest number served is the same?

13. pp. 39-40: Is necrophilia a moral issue or simply an unusual personal preference? Why or why not?

14. p. 40:   Is a theory of human nature a hidden assumption behind utilitarianism?

15. pp. 41-42: What is another example of the difference between internal and external goods?

16. pp. 41-42: Do you have to be virtuous to experience the internal goods of practices?

17. p. 42:   Are external rewards corrupting medicine?

18. pp. 42-44: Do colleges confuse the internal and external goods in sports? Is that a problem?

19. p. 43:   Are external goods more effective motivators than internal goods? Must they be in this society?

20. p. 45:   Can you be a virtuous person and not get "stepped on?"

21. pp. 46-47: Is it true that vice is easier if you are in a job for external rewards?

22. p. 48:   Is this discussion of business and home accurate?

Saturday

Mary Ann Meyer, Jim Andrews and Dave O'Brien

Meyer: Dave, you mentioned last evening that you wanted to talk about the relationship of rights and virtue theory.

O'Brien: Yes. I wanted to sit down with philosophers from the conference who've put some thought into these issues. There were several presentations during the conference that dealt with rights. I really like that approach in my work and on the hospital ethics committee. For one thing it gives a basis for respect in the physician-patient relationship. Each party has a right to be respected. For another, rights are relatively clear. A person's right to make decisions about his or her own body is basic and certain actions follow from that, truth-telling by the doctor, for example.

Andrews: There's some debate in philosophy about where rights come from though I see your point. Your example about respect and truth-telling has some roots in Kant.

O'Brien: Didn't he argue that we should respect each other because we're all rational?

Andrews: Basically yes. If you have a patient and you recognize that the person is also a rational being, you would be inconsistent to lie to the person or to show disrespect. Kant argues that we have duties to each other because we are all rational beings.

O'Brien: I think there's a lot of truth in that. I remember an article I read once that I think originally was in *Harper's Magazine* in 1927. It was by a physician named Joseph Collins. Collins argued that physicians ought to learn how to lie well, that most people can't handle bad news. It was really utilitarian because Collins kept implying that the greatest good in many situations is brought about by lying to the patient. You should see the response to that article now! People go through the roof.

Andrews: Fear of malpractice suits?

O'Brien: Probably some, but I really think the main reason is that physicians recognize patients as being rational people who deserve respect. There's an understanding of the dignity associated with that. If I lie to my patients, even if I think it's somehow good for them, I'm really putting them down as people.

Meyer: That's a good modern way of putting Kant's point. But let me raise something that I've seen used against Kant. Wouldn't you say sometimes that you could accept lying in certain situations? Say you give a placebo to a patient who is constantly in your office with no physical problem. A placebo is really a lie. Couldn't you say that lying is OK for **any** physician in that case, or, in fact, for any rational person?

O'Brien: No.

Meyer: Why?

O'Brien: Because it's not just a matter of saying anyone can do it in that case. That's not the point. The most important thing is respect for the rationality of the patient. People who constantly need placebos are usually not physically sick but have some psychological need. Now I can say, "Well, he's not rational so I can lie to him" or I can say "Underneath this problem is a rational person so I will insist on treating him with respect." What I would do would be help the person see a therapist or counselor. I have to tell him the truth. He does have a problem. It's just not a physical one. The point is to get to the real problem by working with the patient, not cover up the problem with lies or placebos.

Meyer: OK. Here's a tougher case. Let me modify a scene Kant himself mentions. Someone comes into the hospital who has a clear intention of harming a patient there - say he has some grudge against the patient, whatever. That person comes to you and says where is the patient? Do you lie to him? He's clearly rational.

O'Brien: Obviously I'd lie. I'm not going to let him hurt the person.

Meyer: But then is lying OK for anybody in that case? How is that different from the placebo?

O'Brien: Again, let's back up a step. Why should I respect the dignity and rationality of the person who wants to hurt someone and deny the dignity and respect of the patient he's going to hurt? The patient hasn't made any choice to be hurt. He or she has rights too. I guess I would rate the innocent's person's right to live above the truth owed to the questioner. If there's a conflict, I'll go with protecting innocent life. Based on protecting that right to innocent life, I guess I would say that everyone should lie to the questioner. It's better than saying everyone should promote harming innocent people!

Andrews: Isn't your decision based on utilitarianism? A greater good?

O'Brien: Maybe but I'm not sure. I somehow sense the right to live is more basic than the right to the truth.

Meyer: Yes, perhaps there's some sort of logical or human priority here. I suppose you could also argue that by wanting to harm someone or do an immoral act the questioner has somehow waived his right to truth. Some philosophers have argued that. It's a complicated but important issue. But I really like your point about not treating patients with placebos. That's a good Kantian response.

Andrews: But in your practice, Dave, are there **any** people you don't consider rational whom you don't think have rights?

O'Brien: Sure but that takes a great deal of knowledge and study about the person. Clearly there are psychotic individuals who are not rational at all. But before I would go over that line of mutual dignity, I would make darn sure all efforts to be rational fail. Even then I would respect the person as another human being.

Meyer: On what basis? Kant says rationality is the basis for mutual respect.

O'Brien: But I also share suffering with other people. Just because someone's not rational doesn't mean I can do what I want to him.

Andrews: Yes, that's a point raised by philosophers arguing for animal rights. I can be just as inconsistent by torturing an animal as by denying your respect as a rational being. I know what suffering is. I have no grounds for causing you suffering when I know I would not want that myself. I think what you're saying is that even with patients who are clearly not rational a kind of Kantian point still holds. It might be necessary to lie to keep a dangerously psychotic person from harming himself or others but there are elements of being human besides rationality so you have to treat him with as much respect as possible.

O'Brien: I agree and all this makes great sense to me but what on earth does it have to do with virtue theory? The two approaches seem to be in different worlds.

Meyer: Let me ask you, Dave, why should I respect your rights?

O'Brien: I thought we just covered that. We're both rational and deserve dignity and respect.

Meyer: Yeah but say I don't care about that. So what? We're both rational - big deal. If I feel like lying to you, I'll lie to you.

Andrews: I think maybe what Mary Ann's getting at is that liars lie to people. They don't really care about your rationality, your suffering or anything else.

O'Brien: So the kind of person you are makes a big difference.

Meyer: Exactly. Someone with certain character traits will not care about respecting your rights. They might intellectually know you are rational or whatever but it has no effect on their actions. What I'm getting at is that a virtuous character seems to be assumed in rights theories in certain ways.

Andrews: Recognizing something is not the same as acting on it.

Meyer: Yes. I've thought about this issue a lot and I think you can split people into four groups on this point. Some people may not even recognize that they share a common humanity. They are completely blind to other people's dignity.

Andrews: Psychopaths?

Meyer: Yes. But I think some psychopaths might fit the second group. Some people may recognize a common humanity and know others deserve respect but rarely if ever act on that knowledge. They just don't care. They have very little of what we would call empathy or sensitivity. I think both these first two groups show signs of real vices or defects in people.

O'Brien: I'd agree with that.

Meyer: Still others may be basically decent people and want to respect someone else but can't bring themselves to do it at times - that might be a form of *akrasia*. I suspect that's the most common reason rights are violated. You know your neighbor or the clerk in the store deserves the truth and usually you're a decent, moral person, but this one time you lie or violate the person's right to privacy - something like that. Finally, you have the people who recognize rights and consistently act on them. They're the ideal people that rights theorists talk about. Their desires are already developed into strong virtuous habits.

Andrews: I was just thinking of an example of what Mary Ann was saying that goes on all the time in the world. Alan Gewirth, a contemporary ethicist, argues that we're all aware of the need for freedom because we all know what voluntariness is like. We all choose and make decisions about our life - we all regard our freedom as good. One of the origins of the shared right to basic freedom lies in that awareness. I think Gewirth is right. But at present there are plenty of places in the world where basic freedoms are denied. And I would bet that in most of those cases the tyrant or torturers know that they are violating something we all share as human beings - the desire for freedom. But they just don't care. Their characters are such that they're closed off to the respect and dignity owed to other human beings.

O'Brien: So how would this apply to my field?

Meyer: Recognizing rights is a big step forward in medicine.

The idea that doctors ought to be liars should be put to rest. But the character of the physician is important. Deep habits are critical to how we act. If a medical student learns that patients have rights but at the same time has little or no empathy for people, he or she may respect rights only for external reasons - like in Jim's example of fear of lawsuits - and not because of genuine respect for the other person. This opens the door to possible abuse of rights if the situation changes. Like we mentioned yesterday, if it all depends on external factors, if those factors change, what's to prevent abuse? The two theories - virtues and rights - are complementary.

O'Brien: So, besides rights theories needing virtues, I assume you're saying then that virtuous people need to use the idea of rights too?

Meyer: Yes.   The philosopher Louis Lombardi talks about universal and special moral obligations. Universal obligations apply to everyone at all times. Special obligations apply, for example, in certain roles.   Say you have a decent character and you get into a profession like medicine. In medicine, Lombardi argues, and I'm sure you'd agree, there are special moral obligations such as strict confidentiality. Patients have a right to expect confidentiality between themselves and their doctors.   A virtuous physician who wants to do the best for the patient might not think or use the word "right" but clearly something is going on here besides utilitarianism.   It's not just a matter of saying to yourself, "Well, I guess I better not talk about this patient at the cocktail party because it might have bad results."   There's something about respect for the patient - call it a right or whatever - that blocks public disclosure of that person's personal problems **from the beginning**. To anyone with a decent character these facts about the other person's need for respect guide the behavior of the person. Without that you might have virtuous people trying to do good and doing a lot of harm. I don't know anyone who could **be** a virtuous person and ignore the obligations, duties and rights of different situations.

Andrews: I don't know. Maybe you could be virtuous and be a total utilitarian in action.

Meyer: I doubt it. Rights and duties are an important and I think critical way of expressing virtue. Good people don't function in a void. They need guidelines. I can't conceive of the virtue of justice without some concept of mutual respect and dignity. Aristotle's point that just people do just actions is correct up to a point but, when it comes down to figuring out what "just" means, it has to do with respect, equal distribution, things like that.

O'Brien: While you were talking I was thinking about cases where people who claim to be doing good do violate rights. There were physicians in the Nazi death camps working for the Nazis. Let's say they actually had some empathy for patients. But they supported a demonic institution.

Andrews: Other examples might be the Nazi guards in those camps or the Ku Klux Klan. What if a Klan member was really courageous for the Klan cause? Put his life on the line, that sort of thing. Such people are being courageous for a bad end. A person could violate lots of rights and still be virtuous in certain ways. I think being virtuous for bad ends might be a problem for the theory.

Meyer: I think the key, Jim, was your phrase, "virtuous in certain ways." I would argue that the answer to that problem isn't the virtues the person has; it's the virtues the person doesn't have.

O'Brien: A courageous Nazi guard wasn't virtuous enough?

Meyer: Right. So the guard could be courageous. What about empathy or sensitivity?

Andrews: But some of those people were caring fathers at home and brutal killers in the camps. They had empathy. They simply defined the people in the camp out of their range of action.

Meyer: If I give one dollar out of a thousand to charity, I'm generous but not much. If I drink to the point of mild but not debilitating drunkenness, I'm a little temperate but not much. My desires are minimally trained for that virtue. Same way for those guards. I actually think some of them were completely lacking in certain key virtues. They were psychopaths in the perfect job for someone who's blind to human dignity or who has no empathy for the suffering of other people. Others may have had some degree of empathy but not much. I read something once that ties into this. *Newsweek* ran the recollections of a 100-year-old woman who earlier in her life was in Bergen-Belsen Concentration Camp where Anne Frank died. The camp commander had some pre-war experience with a relative of hers so she was made "leader" and he showed some empathy for her. He had a very small amount of this character trait but not enough to make him recognize or act on the suffering he was causing all around him. A more fully virtuous person acts virtuously in different situations. The fact that some virtues can be used to violate rights is the result of some other important virtues that are missing or barely present.

O'Brien: OK, but you mentioned the virtuous person knows how to act in different situations. How does a person learn how to do that? Is there a certain virtue that tells you which virtue is best in a situation? That kind of trait would seem to be always good.

Meyer: Aristotle thought so. He said there was a character trait that guides other character traits - a kind of wisdom.   Prudence or practical wisdom are terms sometimes given to it. The Greek term, which I prefer, is *phronesis*.

O'Brien: I think of "prudence" as a practical matter, not moral. You know, like how much coffee I should drink.

Meyer: It was practical for the Greeks too but it also had a much stronger moral angle than it has now. People with *phronesis* are able to step back and see when it's good to exercise other virtues.   They're also good judges of what the mean is in different situations. Aristotle calls this an intellectual virtue - a virtue of the mind. It's not a direct action virtue like courage or temperance or generosity but it guides the use of the practical virtues. I have my students give examples. Is it good to develop friendship with certain people? Is this charity asking for money an important one? Or, if I do give, how much should I give?   Should I be courageous and tell the boss what I think? Or, if I do think it is good to tell him, what would be the appropriate way to do it?   *Phronesis* is both about selection of virtues and about finding the mean for different virtues in different circumstances.

O'Brien: So there's a kind of absolute virtue.   I guess there might be times when a person **shouldn't** think of what to do in a situation because it would take too much time but a person with a highly developed sense of what you call *phronesis* would even know when to do that.   He or she would have a sort of pre-reflective sensitivity to situations.

Meyer: I'd agree.   I think *phronesis* is always a virtue regardless of the situation. It's the character trait that allows a person to do what's best in the variety of shifting situations in life, a sort of inner moral navigator. I think it's also essential to rights theories.

O'Brien: How?

Meyer: Sometimes rights should not be respected. How do you determine when they should or should not be? Let me give you a personal example. I have a teenager in the family who's very good at expressing rights claims, especially about freedom of hours and freedom of movement. There's no question that an adult asking for such freedoms deserves to have their rights respected. And there's no question that a 5-year-old's demands would have to be taken with a grain of salt. But what does a person do with a 16-year-old? It's a tough decision and whether or not the right should be respected is a matter of a certain kind of sensitivity on my part, something I work at but often fail to achieve. That sensitivity is a form of *phronesis* - knowing when to respect rights and when not to.

O'Brien: But you could argue that such a right doesn't exist for a 5-year-old and may not for a 16-year-old. It's not a matter of whether or not to respect it. It's a matter of whether it exists.

Andrews: Yes, but that's not a real criticism of Mary Ann's point. If you want to put it that way, then the dilemma is whether or not the right exists and *phronesis* is still needed to deal with that question.

O'Brien: I think I know another example of what you mean. Many physicians talk about respecting rights but I have one colleague whose idea of respecting a patient's right to knowledge is to overload the person with information, often without considering the patient's feelings in the situation. I think several of his patients have been traumatized by having their rights respected.

Meyer: I see that as another form of *phronesis* applied, or, in your example, not applied to rights. I think too there's another intellectual virtue that has a lot to do with rights. There's a character trait I call openness to truth, the willingness to be open to wherever the evidence may lead. If a person does not have a certain degree of openness to truth, then another person's right will not even be recognized. Evidence about the other person will be ignored or suppressed. Without the virtue of openness to truth, rights theories can't function at all.

Andrews: So how is that different from the empathy or sensitivity you just mentioned? That seems to be openness to truth.

Meyer: They're close but I don't think they're the same. Empathy I would argue is more of a practical virtue. If I see someone obviously suffering and fail to act, I may be lacking in empathy. But imagine someone raised to believe that all the members of some immigrant group are lazy or unintelligent. They run into plenty of examples to counter that and may even be aware of studies that show the stereotype wrong, but they refuse to recognize the evidence. I think that's more than lack of empathy. It also has to do with an intellectual vice - a failure to recognize and accept evidence. That's what I'm getting at.

O'Brien: Smoking may be another good example. People deny that evidence all the time. That doesn't have much to do with lack of empathy.

Meyer: Yes.

O'Brien: So physicians like the tactless one I mentioned are deficient in some character trait?

Meyer: I think you can make a good case for that. I'm not sure it's openness to truth in that case - it could be - but it sounds more like the person doesn't have empathy for the patient's situation. It's nothing like the extreme cases we discussed earlier, but the person you mentioned does seem to be lacking some sensitivity.

O'Brien: I still have trouble seeing how virtue would apply to most of my day-to-day work as a physician. I can see where developing certain character traits would make a doctor more sensitive to patients. And I can see where a virtue like *phronesis* is important as a background to my practice. But medicine these days is mainly a matter of proper technique. Most people I see don't care about my character but they care a lot about how competent I am. Competent technique in medicine is a matter of training and intelligence, not character. The benevolent small town physician is becoming history. I'd rather be operated on by a highly competent egoist than by an incompetent saint.

Meyer: I'd agree that some of the traditional virtues in medicine have gone by the wayside but I don't think competence exists in a vacuum. To develop and maintain competence in medicine requires certain character traits - diligence, hard work, self-discipline, several others. Even if someone is completely self-centered in personal relationships, if they're going to remain competent in a field like medicine, they're going to need enough self-discipline to keep up in their field and do careful work in their medical practice.

Andrews: So you're saying different virtues are at work?

Meyer: Yes. I agree with Dave's point about technique. I think the ideal many doctors have today is based less on personal relationships and more on excellence in technique. I suspect specialization has a lot to do with that. What that ideal does is bring out certain virtues that may have been less significant in the days of the country doctor. So I think virtues are just as important in medical practice today but they are ones that fit highly specialized and urbanized medicine.

O'Brien: I take it you're granting my point about virtue not being directly practical in day-to day work.

Meyer: Yes and no. You wouldn't have physicians respecting
                    rights without certain character traits in the
                    background and you wouldn't have competence in
                    medicine without certain other virtues in the
                    background. Your highly competent egoist wouldn't be
                    highly competent if he couldn't forget himself long
                    enough to keep himself sharp in his field.   To that
                    extent he's not a pure egoist. Being in the background
                    doesn't mean virtues aren't important.

O'Brien: This change in emphasis toward technique has caused
                    some real soul-searching on our ethics committee.
                    We've had some cases that forced us to face the issue of
                    what exactly health is. High-tech medicine has caused
                    us a lot of ethical problems.

Andrews: You mean like keeping people alive with machines?

O'Brien: Yes, but I was thinking more of conflicts between
                    technology and personal care. Is it better to die at
                    home with loved ones even if the technical care is not
                    as good? Should the hospital have a more integrated
                    approach to patients so they feel less like a number in
                    the computer? All issues we've faced, often more than
                    once.

Andrews: Have philosophers been any help?

O'Brien: Quite a bit, though it often depended on the case. Both
                    the utilitarian and rights approaches have helped to
                    clarify some of the key issues involved. And
                    philosophers are good at making distinctions. One of
                    the reasons I wanted to chat with you was to see
                    whether you thought virtue theory might be helpful to
                    us on the committee.

Meyer: I'm not sure. One of the ideas MacIntyre discusses is
                    how people view their lives as narratives and how we
                    make sense of events in life by putting them into a
                    story-line. That might relate to your committee's

discussion about how patients and hospitals handle illness or death.

O'Brien: Maybe.   People go through a kind of psychological disintegration when they become severely ill or injured and especially when they become aware that they're going to die.   Their life doesn't fit together anymore. I guess in MacIntyre's terms the story no longer makes sense.

Meyer: Maybe that's where the medical staff plays a critical role. Putting the story back together.

O'Brien: Our committee has discussed the fact that high tech alone doesn't help in this regard. Injured or ill people need other people who care - family, staff, clergy.

Meyer: Sounds like the loss of some traditional virtues in medicine has had negative results. I can think of one way virtue theory might be useful to your committee. Maybe it can help you think about how to bring integrity back to patients' lives in this time of specialized medicine. How can a hospital help patients put their lives back together, not just physically but psychologically?   Maybe it wouldn't hurt for your committee to talk about what your goal is for a flourishing human being.

O'Brien: It would seem awfully vague to discuss what a flourishing human being is without a concrete case in front of us. It sounds like the sort of thing you get in advertising brochures for the hospital.

Meyer: Sure but it's also a fact that medicine has always worked with some concept of human flourishing. I think nowadays it's pretty much limited to physical health. But I think that model may be changing - the emphasis now on the relationship of mental stress to physical health, for example. I don't think it's vague to sit down and talk about what kind of human being is the goal of your practice.

O'Brien: Um, yes. There just seem to be a lot of possible goals in medicine.

Meyer: But that's true of my profession too. Different departments have different goals. The degree of specialization at a university is incredible. We've had discussion about this between departments. For us the underlying issue is what exactly we are trying to do in educating students. What is excellence as a human being? I think that anybody who claims to be an educator at any level ought to seriously think about that. I suspect the situation is similar in medicine. You're trying to heal people, help them flourish. Do you have any positive idea about what that goal means? Is it only physical health?

O'Brien: But there's really a big difference between education and medicine. Educators are moving people forward, so to speak. We're trying to bring people back to a certain baseline. Discussion of goals is much more important in your case. In our case the human body sets our goals.

Meyer: Yes but those bodies have emotions and dreams and complex psychologies. It might not hurt for more doctors to think about what an all-round healthy person is.

O'Brien: Well, I'll carry your point to the committee to see what their response is. I suspect it will be something like "nice idea, but no time." Speaking of time, I'm afraid I have to be going. I wish I could have been here the first evening. This has been most interesting.

Meyer: I agree. I have a lot to think about when I get back. It's been very enjoyable.

Andrews: Yes, it was a pleasure meeting you.

O'Brien: Thanks. I'll let you know what my committee thinks of some of the ideas we discussed.

Meyer: Bye.

Andrews: My plane leaves shortly, Mary Ann. It's been really good seeing you again and having a chance to talk.

Meyer: Yes. Maybe we can keep in touch more by e-mail.

Andrews: I'll make a point of it. Take care.

Meyer: Thanks, Jim. You too. Have a safe flight.

Discussion Questions

1. pp. 54-55: Should a physician ever lie to a patient?

2. p. 55: O'Brien is claiming that the right to live is more basic than the right to truth. Are there any **logical** grounds that the right to live is more basic?

3. pp. 55-56: Does a person who wants to do an immoral act waive his or her right to the truth?

4. p. 56: Do psychotic individuals have moral rights? What are some? Where do they come from?

5. p. 56: Does a tiger have rights? A frog? An insect? Why or why not?

6. pp. 57-58: Is it true that a virtuous character is critical for acting on rights?

7. p. 58: Do you think Andrews is correct that most tyrants or torturers know that they are violating the rights of their victims?

8. p. 59: Is confidentiality in the physician-patient relationship an absolute right? Should it ever be broken?

9. p. 60: Could you be a virtuous person and not use the concept of "rights?" Remember that "right" is a fairly recent concept in Western history.

10. pp. 60-61: Does Meyer have an adequate answer as to why virtues like courage can be used for harmful ends?

11. pp. 62-63: Is *phronesis* the same as what we call today common sense? Or is it more than that?

12. pp. 62-63: Is Aristotle right that *phronesis* is a separate virtue, that is, a special kind of intellectual ability?

13. pp. 63-64: Is openness to truth always a virtue?

14. p. 64:   What are some reasons why people refuse to accept evidence?

15. pp. 64-65: Is the character of a physician irrelevant in medicine today?

16. pp. 65-66: Is medicine today less concerned with virtues than in the past or is it concerned with different virtues?

17. pp. 66-67: Is it a hospital's responsibility to help patients psychologically put their lives back together?

18. p. 68:   Is O'Brien right that setting goals is more important for educators than for health care workers?

Part II

Awards Ceremony

Setting: Awards ceremony at the local branch of the state university a year after the previous conversations. Professor Meyer is receiving an award for excellence in teaching. Her friend, Jim Andrews, hears about the award and attends the ceremony. Afterwards they meet for coffee in the school cafeteria. The talk turns to the relationship of doing well and being honored for it.

Andrews: I imagine you must have been proud to be up there. Given the size of your faculty, not many people have that chance.

Meyer: I was proud but I kept wondering whether I should be. When I was growing up, I was taught that humility's a virtue and that even if you do achieve something you shouldn't let pride take over.

Andrews: Sounds like your religious upbringing.

Meyer: It was. The point was that no matter what you do you're nothing compared to the greatness of God. My mother used to say I should always keep that in mind. When she heard I was going to go to graduate school and become a philosopher she gave me a special warning against intellectual pride. That was a sin.

Andrews: I was never raised religiously but I have some of the same feelings when people praise me for something - like somehow I don't deserve it.

Meyer: From what I know now as a philosopher I think both our feelings are irrational. If a person does well, why shouldn't they be honored for it and why shouldn't they **enjoy** the honor? I'm angry at myself because instead of enjoying what went on today I kept having self-doubts. Aristotle wouldn't have had any.

Andrews: Who knows? At least he writes like he wouldn't have any. If he's right, the excellent person not only deserves to be honored but has the right to expect it. That's really different from the way we were raised.

Meyer: And I think healthier. If a person is a great tennis player why shouldn't he expect to be honored for that? I don't think Aristotle meant that a great tennis player should be honored as a great human being. The person may not be very skilled in other areas and may not even be very virtuous. But as a tennis player, go for it. The problem with this society is that we confuse skills and character traits all the time. A terrific football player is assumed to be some special kind of person outside of playing football. We sure know that's wrong.

Andrews: And the person may be confused himself.

Meyer: Sure. After enough people tell you how great you are, you start to forget that the only reason they say that is because you are good at a sport. That's what Aristotle meant by false pride or vanity.

Andrews: I can see deserving honor but I guess I have some problem with the idea of expecting honor. No matter how you cut it that seems awfully self-centered. You just got a teaching award and it was well-deserved. But if you expected or looked for that honor wouldn't that take away from the teaching itself? It seems to be too much concern with social approval.

Meyer: I see your point. Aristotle thought a person could separate the two things and look at it more objectively. Teaching is teaching. If you do a good job you should expect honor for it. He himself says that the person who focuses on getting honor instead of the behavior leading to the honor is no longer virtuous. It's like the Pharisee story in the New Testament. If you replace good actions with a desire for the honors involved in doing good, your motive has changed and you'll do whatever's necessary to get more honor.

Andrews: But looking for or expecting honor seems to lead to phoniness automatically.

Meyer: I don't think so. I think it depends on how the honor relates to what you're doing. There's an example I talk about with my students. Anyone in any profession or craft has a peer group. If I'm an architect and I design a really impressive building I would expect some admiration from my fellow architects. It's natural and healthy because the procedures of architecture are understood by my peer group. Doing architecture can be done in better or worse ways. Everybody knows that. I'm expecting honor for doing my job well but that doesn't make me an egoist or a hypocrite. It's a natural follow-up to being part of a shared group.

Andrews: But what you mean by honor seems a little different than getting an award.

Meyer: Sure but my point was that Aristotle was correct that expecting honor for a job well done is a perfectly natural and healthy thing to do for anyone involved in any shared activity. It's not vanity or false pride. If that honor includes a trophy or a monetary award, great. Enjoy it. Just don't make that the dominant goal. I guess it's easier to lose perspective if the award is some public event but Aristotle's point still holds.

Andrews: OK. I'll buy for the time being that expecting honor from a peer group seems natural. But I think what you said about your mother points out something important. Her firm belief in God means that no pride or honor is ever fully justified. From that angle even a great architect doesn't deserve honor. As an architect she is simply using the ability that God gave her. So I'm not really sure expecting honor is so natural after all. I think it depends on what assumption you make about life.

Meyer: My mom might not like to hear me say this but I think she's wrong about pride. Look at the early history of Christianity or look at those groups today that claim to be the purest Christians. Don't they honor their heroes?

Andrews: Sure. So what?

Meyer: Because it proves my point. Imagine you stand up for your belief in a hostile world against tyrants, persecution, whatever. Imagine that you even are willing to be martyred for it. If you face danger, don't you think it must be worth doing that?

Andrews: I wouldn't do it otherwise.

Meyer: And who defines this worth? Your community of believers. So wouldn't you expect to be respected and honored for your courage by your community?

Andrews: I see what you're getting at. Even those groups that claim you should always be humble honor those who live this way of life. Aristotle's soldiers may have marched through Athens to great honor but the Christian martyrs or saints are spoken of reverently or maybe people carry their pictures around. So honor for virtue is natural there too.

Meyer: Right.

Andrews: But if honor is so universal for people we admire, I wonder why so many people in this society think that seeking honor for achievements is arrogance and vanity.

Meyer: Partly what we mentioned earlier.   People get
              confused. They achieve something like a new record
              in a sport and then they think they deserve more honor
              than they do. And the rest of us assume right off the
              bat that anybody expecting honor is expecting too
              much. I think the media has a lot to do with it. The
              way we turn people into "stars" makes it hard to
              distinguish what people deserve from what they don't.

Andrews: So what we need in this society isn't more humility but
              a better distinction about what deserves honor and
              what doesn't.

Meyer: That's one way of putting it.   Another might be that
              people should be humble about what they deserve to be
              humble about and expect honor where they deserve it.
              Keep your life in perspective. But I'm not optimistic
              about that. The media needs to sell papers and TV
              programs. So they sensationalize people to sell their
              product and everybody gets confused because of it.
              Parents and teachers who want to help young people
              keep their lives in focus end up fighting a system that
              promotes confusion about character.

Andrews: Or else parents succumb to it too and start thinking of
              their children as successful human beings if they make
              a lot of money or get famous.

Meyer: Right.

Andrews: I have to give a talk to a group of elementary school
              teachers in a couple weeks on ethics and teaching and
              some of this is relevant to the research I've been doing.
              I can see some connections between character issues in
              ethics and what parents and teachers are trying to do
              for children.

Meyer: You mean about developing their potential?

Andrews: Yes, but more than that. What exactly are we trying to achieve when we teach kids morality? If you think about it, we often sound like utilitarians and Kantians when we talk ethics with them. We tell them to respect the rights of others, remind them of their duties to other people, and encourage them to care for the good of all. But what's our goal in talking that way to children?

Meyer: Habit formation?

Andrews: Right and that's what virtue ethics is all about - habits and character formation. That's going to be the focus of my talk to the teachers. What we're trying to do for children is to get them into the habit of certain feelings like empathy and help them learn certain decision procedures so that when they're older they'll automatically care about other people and the rights of others. Since kids don't have developed characters yet, teachers and parents are molding those habits.

Meyer: I was thinking of some neighbors of mine. They have a son who was never disciplined. He's been a real problem in the neighborhood ever since I moved there. When he was younger he was never given any guidance or limitations and now that he's a young adult his life is a mess. He goes through relationships with females with almost no ability to care about the other person. Police seem to be at our neighbor's house about once a month because their son has no respect for others' property. His desires and emotions have no internal compass. He's never developed habits of character that are stable and productive.

Andrews: Poor parenting and a weak moral character seem to go together.

Meyer: Yes and that combination can make life hell for other people. It's another example of character having utilitarian effects - in this case negative.

Andrews: I like the distinction psychologists make between permissive, authoritarian and authoritative parents.

Meyer: I understand permissive. That's my neighbor. What's the difference in the other two?

Andrews: I think permissive and authoritarian would be the extremes. Aristotle might say that permissive parents can't discipline their own emotions and maybe lack courage to discipline their children. On the other hand, authoritarian parents use rigid rules that are rarely explained. They have habits of desire that are inflexible and not subject to reason. With anger, permissive parents may not get angry enough at the appropriate times; authoritarian parents get too angry too often and frequently at the wrong times and in the wrong ways. They often discipline children with physical pain of some sort and usually without much explanation. The effect on the child is almost always negative. The children of authoritarian parents obey laws when an authority is around and they look law-abiding. But they're often hostile and resentful people who have poor impulse control. They strike out at people they don't like. As adults they respond to external authority when it's present but don't have self-discipline about their own desires when the authority's not there.

Meyer: So what is authoritative parenting?

Andrews: Parents whose character is probably a good example of Aristotle's mean. They have rational guidance of their own desires and enough practical wisdom to judge situations accurately. They supply guidelines and limits for children but explain the reasons for the discipline. They also recognize children's need to explore and make their own mistakes. They get angry when appropriate in the right degree and in productive ways. The anger is based on a deep love for the child, not their own self-centered needs. Evidence shows that this is the most effective way to help a child build good character traits.

Meyer: So authoritative parents tend to have happier and more stable children because the kids themselves develop habits of justice, habits of caring and so on.

Andrews: Right. Our society as a whole can't seem to figure that out. They set up a false dilemma between permissive on the one hand and discipline on the other. You hear politicians talking all the time about the permissive society but usually the other side is authoritarianism. Neither extreme is helpful and both can turn out some very destructive human beings.

Meyer: I suppose you're going to argue that teaching can fit into the same categories.

Andrews: Yes, to a degree. A third grade teacher can be too permissive and a class can be chaos. Or she can be too authoritarian in which case the child obeys while the teacher is threatening discipline but the kid doesn't care much for what's really happening in the class. Or the teacher can keep limits and provide guidance while explaining reasons in a caring environment. It all stems from the teacher's own character traits - his or her own ability to find the mean in emotions and desires and to be able to judge situations appropriately.

Meyer: I think many teachers are frustrated because they do try to teach in the way you mentioned but it doesn't work.

Andrews: Kids won't respond a lot of times because their homes are not like that and even by third grade they've developed some negative character traits. Teachers can't directly teach virtue itself - I guess Socrates was right. But what they can do, or at least try to do, is set up an environment so children can develop habits of respect, understanding and other important traits.

Meyer: Right, but easier said than done. A teacher only has the children a limited amount of time and helping them learn appropriate patterns of desires and emotions is a tall order.

Andrews: Yes. I can hear the teachers' questions now. How can I teach a child what "appropriate" is for future circumstances? How can I go against a bad home environment?

Meyer: I guess one of the things that might help is that a lot of children identify with teachers to some degree. Kids can learn to moderate their desires and passions by modeling on their teacher's responses. If a child learns to think about the most appropriate response when they're young then, when they're adults, they'll be used to doing that. No guarantees but it's a lot easier if your teachers cared about you and helped you when you were younger.

Andrews: But what if I choose appropriately but don't do well at what I choose? I've been thinking about a child who decides to try out for volleyball. She loves the game and her parents think it would be healthy for her but when she does it she's not very good at it. Teachers run into this a lot. Children who personally make a good choice but are defeated by the project.

Meyer: That seems to be part of growing up. We all learn from our mistakes.

Andrews: Sure but I'm thinking about kids whose self-image is shot because they're not very good athletes or debaters or whatever. These things are supposed to be fun but can be really harmful.

Meyer: I think that's a distortion of what those events are about. It's the difference between external and internal goods again. MacIntyre points out that internal goods are not in limited supply but external goods are. There are only so many trophies. That distinction seems really important to children's activities. Schools need to emphasize the joy of the sport and not be so concerned with the prize. Some schools in my area go crazy over adding to their trophy case.

Andrews: I think that's a national trend.

Meyer: Yeah and a sad one. It's just like the honor issue we started with today. Excellence deserves to be honored and I'll stand by that but when the emphasis is too heavy on the external goal a person can lose sight of the internal joys of the practice. The more you emphasize these external rewards the more a child will be crushed if he or she isn't good at it. In fact I can see how that could actually teach a child to cheat. Who cares about how well you play? Let's get that award.

Andrews: I'm trying to think how I would make that point to the teachers. Part of the art of teaching is to help children with mediocre skills or abilities enjoy what they're doing. That really goes against that "star" quality we mentioned earlier. If you don't win, you've failed as a person. Our society preaches that in many subtle and not so subtle ways.

Meyer: Yes. I'm constantly struck by the number of college students who think that almost all human practices have ulterior motives relating to money or fame or ego. It's not hard to see how this develops in children. I guess a simple example is Christmas. Most of the talk about Christmas is about virtues like generosity and empathy but in practice the focus in this society is on getting the latest gadgets or toys for yourself. Same in athletics. People talk about character building but athletes who are pure egoists are considered heroes and are seen advertising shoes or game equipment. Even in personal relationships TV teaches kids that friendship between the sexes usually has some ulterior sexual motive. It's no wonder so many adults think some self-centered reward is the ulterior motive behind everything people do.

Andrews: But we're not going to get rid of trophies or Christmas presents or sex or awards for teaching, for that matter. Not sure I'd want to.

Meyer: Neither would I. Maybe what parents and teachers need to do is help children appreciate both aspects - the joy of playing a game **and** the desire for the trophy. Help kids keep things in the right perspective. A trophy can be a great motivation but it should never get in the way of simply enjoying the game.

Andrews: I agree with your point about perspective. That should help in my presentation. I have to be heading out, Mary Ann. As usual it's been great fun talking with you. And I think you really deserved that teaching award.

Meyer: Thanks, Jim. Good luck with your talk. Let me know how it goes.

Andrews: I will. Take care.

Discussion Questions

1. p. 74: Should great tennis players be humble about their ability?

2. pp. 74-75: Does looking for or expecting honor lead necessarily to egoism or hypocrisy?

3. pp. 76-77: Does the media distort the concept of "honor" in our society? Or is Meyer's claim unfair to the media?

4. pp. 78-79: How much of children's poor moral character is the fault of parents?

5. p. 79: Should future parents be forced in some way to take parenting classes?

6. pp. 79-80: Is permissiveness the major source of problem children in our society? Or is the term simply a political catchword?

7. pp. 80-81: Can a teacher teach virtue? If yes, how? If no, why not?

8. pp. 81-82: Is the perspective on success discussed in the dialogue a problem in elementary schools today? Or is the issue overstated?

Conference on Feminism and Ethics

Setting: A month later - a conference on feminism and ethics is being held at the university. Small group discussions are scheduled after each presentation. After a talk on the ethics of care given by a well-known feminist philosopher, a discussion group forms consisting of Professor Susan McMillan who teaches feminist philosophy, Professor John Patterson from the anthropology department, Professor Sharon Rice from the psychology department and Professor Meyer who teaches the general ethics courses.

Patterson: I think I understand better now what philosophers mean by feminist ethics. It has to do with an increased appreciation of nurturance and caring, what the speaker called relational ethics.

McMillan: Actually it's a much broader idea than that. Not all feminists agree. There are feminists who argue that way but others who say that emphasizing caring simply is a way of keeping an oppressive system in place.

Patterson: But all cultures need nurturance for their children and some caring between family members.

McMillan: Yes but in Western culture women's role has been defined by caring and that's been used as a way to keep women out of positions of political and economic responsibility. What better caring phrase is there than "A woman's place is in the home." Some feminists think that making caring into an ethical ideal perpetuates a system where men make all the power decisions while women do the nurturing.

Meyer: But I think the point of the lecture was to expand the concept of caring into the whole population, not to isolate it to women. The point was to help men recognize caring as an important part of their lives too.

McMillan: True but I still wonder whether all this nurturance talk deflects from the fact that we live in a power-stratified society. A lot of men might say, "Sure, I'll care more but I'm still going to make the decisions."

Meyer: Some might do that but I think if a person is serious about becoming a more empathetic person then being a self-centered jerk becomes harder.

Patterson: I keep thinking of something Malcolm X said when he was asked about nonviolent protests against racism. "If his language is a gun, get a gun." It's what they understand. I can see Susan's point about how feminists might say the same thing. You don't confront oppression by caring the oppressors into submission. You deal with oppressors by confronting them on their own terms.

Rice: But doesn't that kind of response just validate the whole mess? Pretty soon you've got people at each other's throats. Isn't there a more creative way out of this than meeting fire with fire?

Meyer: I'm not sure the ethics of care is as wimpy as you make it sound. Caring doesn't mean you have to agree with everything. When my daughter wanted every toy in sight, it was because I cared that I **didn't** get them for her. She objected plenty but my action was part of caring.

Rice: Yes. I see it in studies of alcoholism. The spouse who cares forces the issue often at a risk to herself. Agreeing with an alcoholic spouse simply facilitates the problem.

Patterson: But is this situation the same?   Isn't politics a different ball game?

McMillan: It seems that way to me. I'm all for expanding caring into the general population but without a power base I don't think it will change the system.

Meyer: I don't think we can talk about a power base without giving some thought to a different view of being a human being. I mean, if the system is changed, what kind of person are we looking for? How would we treat people differently? That's what the ethics of care is about. If we can pin down why caring is important to being human then we have a basis for attacking the current system.

Patterson: But how would you characterize the current system? It's a tremendously complex culture and I'm not sure there is one "system."

McMillan: I think you can characterize it in broad terms. Our approach to relationships is based on a contract metaphor like in business. We think of ourselves as isolated individuals who have to set up rules in order to relate to each other. The assumption is that without these contracts between people there would be chaos.

Rice: It sounds similar to some of Carol Gilligan's work in psychology. Her studies showed that males tend toward black-white thinking with a big emphasis on rules and what she calls the ethics of justice. Since males have traditionally dominated the positions of power, society as a whole has been led to this way of thinking. But her argument is that this isn't the only way of looking at human relationships or ethical problems. Her research shows that women tend to assume from the beginning an interconnectedness between people. If we are interconnected to begin with, caring or empathy is a more natural way to approach problems.

Meyer: Sharon, I want to pick up on your use of the
              word "natural." Why is it more natural to care than to
              seek revenge, for example? Seeking revenge seems
              natural too.

Rice: I guess what I meant is that caring comes more
              naturally to women than to most men. It sounds
              stereotyped but the evidence is there. Gilligan's point
              is that a mature morality would combine both caring
              and justice.

Patterson: How can a morality be mature or immature? I don't
              think that makes much sense from an anthropologist's
              perspective. Features of human development can be
              mature or immature but a morality?

Rice: I can give you an example. Gilligan's point is that a
              spoiled adult who has no self-control is actually at a
              lower level of development, both psychologically and
              morally, than an adult who reasons and cares about her
              life and her relationships. Egoism is immature
              psychologically and morally.

Patterson: I'll buy the psychological part about immature
              development. That's an empirical issue. But I still
              have problems characterizing a **morality** as
              "immature." It's just different, not better or worse.

Meyer: I think you've hit on a good point, John. I think what's
              happening is that people like Gilligan and Kohlberg
              are tying into a long-standing ethical tradition
              involving character. They're making some assumptions
              about human nature that go beyond the empirical
              studies. I see what they're doing as a modification of
              what Socrates and Aristotle started.

McMillan: That's a twist. Aristotle's view of women was
              incredibly distorted. How is what we're talking about
              related to that?

Meyer: I think the ethics of care and the whole approach of feminism is a necessary historical corrective to virtue ethics. The Greeks had a lot of insights into human character that are just as true today. My students really like many of Aristotle's ideas on friendship and all the talk today about eating well and moderating our desires sounds like Aristotle's idea of temperance. The whole idea of developing excellence continues to be incredibly important in the West.

Rice: So how is the ethics of care an improvement?

Meyer: The Greeks not only had great insights but they had some really big limitations too. The lecture today addressed two of the biggest ones. One was their view of women as second class humans. In some ways Aristotle deserves the most blame for this. Women, he says, are emotional and men are rational; therefore, since reason should govern society, only men are qualified. Men are by nature superior in what makes us uniquely human. But the other related limitation had to do with emotion in general. None of the ancient philosophers thought of emotions on the same par as reason. The argument in the lecture today was that caring or empathy is just as important as reason and that a person who lacks empathy is just as inhumane as one who lacks reason. That makes sense to me and it also shows where Aristotle went wrong. It's not that reason isn't an essential part of being a human being. He's right there. But what he failed to recognize is that the emotional side of us, especially empathy, is also essential.

McMillan: So aren't the people who argue that women are more caring actually supporting the old sexist stereotype? Wouldn't Aristotle buy into that?

Meyer: Well, first I think the jury is out on whether men are less caring or more logical than women in their approach to life. Gilligan's studies indicate tendencies in that direction but her work has been criticized for its cultural bias. Maybe Aristotle was just plain wrong about men being more reason-oriented. It's an empirical question. But, even if there are differences in the sexes, the old stereotype assumed that the differences in fact led to differences in worth as human beings. That's nonsense. You can admit differences in emphasis and recognize both as essential to being human. We've had plenty of reasonable people in our history who didn't have much empathy and I'm sick of seeing the suffering that results. We need more empathy as a species.

Patterson: I'm sitting here as an anthropologist listening to you talk about human nature. I see humans in their concrete cultural setting not as some abstract idea. You're arguing that caring is supposed to be virtuous in some way. I can see how it's important within the family in all cultures. But I have a hard time seeing it as critical in other areas of life.

Rice: Maybe I can suggest one reason why it's important. Social psychologists have found that people who can empathize with each other work better together. Think of a business. If your manager on the job has some sense of empathy for a problem you're facing, odds are better that as an employee you'll feel valued more by the company. Having a boss who cares about you as a person makes a difference in your motivation.

Meyer: One virtue theorist calls what we're talking about having a generous mind. The generous-minded or caring person sees potential where others may see nothing. The caring person can draw out the possibilities in other people. Classic examples are teaching and counseling.

Rice: Yes and caring makes other people feel they're worth something in the process. It can be a business, a family or a classroom.

McMillan: Of course that assumes the structure is fair to begin with. Caring within a business that discriminates against people simply reinforces the unjust structure. Caring puts people to sleep.

Meyer: But again I don't see why caring has to be blind to injustice. Blind empathy is dangerous - I agree. Someone who cared without thinking would be no better off than someone who reasoned without empathy. It's not an argument against caring to point out that people can use it to avoid facing injustices. People can use reason to slaughter innocent people but that's not an argument against reason itself. In fact I think another reason caring is virtuous is that it actually increases the creative potential for the person doing it.

McMillan: How?

Meyer: Take a student as an example. If a student cares about what she is learning, she'll be more motivated to take the material to heart and remember it longer.

Rice: I suspect you mean internalize it.

Meyer: Right. A teacher is the same way. Teachers who care about their discipline will continue to grow in it and those that care about their students will work to set up the best possible learning environment for them.

McMillan: So you're saying a caring person will want to improve an unjust situation because she cares about what she's doing. Maybe so but I still don't find sexist or racist companies being "cared" into changing. It's a power game.

Patterson: But I don't see a conflict between caring and forcing change. When a cultural trait changes, it's often because people cared about the point enough to do something about it. Gandhi loved India and India's people and that was a motivator for his political action. Same for Martin Luther King.

Meyer: Yes. People without empathy are the ones who don't care. And sometimes people have empathy that's too limited. Say somebody works in a racist factory where minorities are verbally assaulted all the time and kept out of good jobs. The person cares about his family but couldn't care less about the minority. What the person needs is more empathy, not less.

Rice: So you agree with Gilligan basically but you're using a different vocabulary than my discipline. You're talking about modifying our definition of a virtuous person.

Meyer: That's it in a nutshell. Philosophy has ignored empathy as a critical virtue and what we're seeing right now is a revolution within ethics. We're moving away from a legalistic approach toward a view that looks at all facets of a human life.

McMillan: I don't know. I see caring all the time in public life. Clerks are caring, politicians are caring, telemarketers care the world for you. Like McDonald's used to say, "We do it all for you." I'm pretty cynical about all this unselfish caring stuff.

Patterson: Yeah, capitalism is a real caring system.

Meyer: Most virtues can be faked - maybe all. People can fake being generous, they can fake courage. Caring's no different. You're right that phony caring is all over the place. Caring is mimicked so often and so well that it becomes really hard to tell the real motivation of people.

Patterson: I often wonder when I'm in a store with a super friendly clerk just how much the clerk cares about me as a customer.

McMillan: My students tell me they're trained to be nice even if they don't want to be. Usually someone who walks in the store is just a potential sale and if clerks aren't friendly or don't look like they care about the customer they won't make the sale. That's why they do it - they don't **really** care.

Meyer: That whole system tends to make young people think that every act of caring has some self-centered motive behind it like profit. I hear that all the time from students. That kind of phony virtue has a bad effect on the society.

Patterson: How? Capitalism seems to be doing fine.

Rice: I suspect I know what Mary Ann's getting at. Studies with children show they pick up on false motives easily. Parents who act like they care but really don't are deceiving their kids. That has a big negative effect on family life.

Meyer: And on other institutions too. Look at the cynicism about politics when every politician makes like they really care about your problem. What they really want is your vote and everybody knows that. So the whole big phony show just increases people's cynical and distrustful attitude toward government. Same with the cynical attitude toward salespeople.

McMillan: But what alternatives do we have?

Meyer: Not many. We seem to have accepted a certain amount of pseudo-caring as inevitable in business and politics. But I'd still argue that an increase in real caring tends to promote everyone's good in the long run.

McMillan: I can see the value of empathy but I keep coming back to my main concern. The empathetic person can be easily exploited. Look at the large number of marriages where the wife keeps "caring" about her husband despite the abuse he gives her. Now I know you said there can be a "tough caring" but where do you draw the line? Caring gets tied too easily to forgiveness and maybe forgiveness is not what should happen in a lot of relationships.

Meyer: But every virtue can lead to exploitation. The generous person can get suckered in by a scam. The courageous person can be tricked by a demagogue into thinking a cause is worth dying for. I don't see why you pick out caring in particular.

McMillan: I think it's a basic problem I have with virtue ethics. It all sounds fine but where are guidelines for action?

Rice: Maybe part of it is balance. That was Gilligan's point. A balanced personality will use reason when appropriate and empathy when appropriate. A balanced personality will know when to lay down the line to another person. It's a kind of psychological maturity based on experience.

Patterson: Is that what Aristotle's famous "mean" is about - balance?

Meyer: Related but not quite the same. The mean refers to moderating our desires. For example, the appropriate amount to eat or drink or the appropriate amount of anger. Gilligan is speaking as a psychologist about the entire personality. It's more of a goal for the whole person.

Rice: Wouldn't balance as a person follow from what Aristotle's talking about?

Meyer: Probably but not necessarily. A person could have virtuous habits in several desires and perhaps still not be well-balanced all-around in Gilligan's sense. It would definitely help to have desires guided by reason if you were shooting for an overall balanced personality. Her idea relates somewhat to what Aristotle calls practical wisdom. A person with practical wisdom knows which virtues to apply and when to do it. In Gilligan's case it would be knowing when to apply justice and when to empathize. But the modern psychological idea of a balanced personality is a broader concept that Aristotle's idea of the mean.

McMillan: Fine, but I still would like to see some clear guidelines for action.

Meyer: Maybe there just aren't always nice clear guidelines. Maybe nature doesn't supply us with those. Part of growing up psychologically is to learn from experience and find the best response in different circumstances. The mature person knows how to be temperate, when to be generous, and how to care in the right place at the right time. Without that ability to learn and modify character there isn't much anyone else can do. You can talk a friend's ear off about stopping herself from being exploited in a relationship but until she herself recognizes the need for a better life she probably won't do much to change the situation.

Patterson: All this talk about balance sounds like an art class.

Rice: Yeah, I was thinking that too. About a month ago I read an article by a couple psychologists who actually claimed a balanced personality **was** beautiful.

Meyer: Haven't heard that angle before.

Rice: Their names are Sabini and Silver. As I recall they said the beauty of a work of art is comparable to the beauty of a person's character.

McMillan: Sounds nice but doesn't say much.

Patterson: Yes, as far as I'm concerned, beauty is in the eye of the beholder as interpreted by the culture's standards. If beauty's analogous to character, so much the worse for character.

Meyer: But it **is** curious. Plato thought beauty and goodness were linked together too. If you look at ethics in the last few hundred years, you almost never find words like harmony or balance. Instead of looking at the picture as a whole, ethicists look at each of the lines in the painting.

Rice: Sabini and Silver point out some interesting similarities. For example, we generally tend to be repelled by cowardice and attracted to courageous people. Why? They claim there's something about the trait of being courageous that strikes an aesthetic chord with us. We somehow feel it fits the human pattern.

McMillan: Well, I do get students often who talk about going beyond superficial looks to the beauty inside a person. That always seems to have a moral dimension when they say it.

Meyer: Yes, like Socrates says. Physical beauty has nothing to do with moral character yet we get trapped by outward appearances. We have to get past that to the character of the person. To him that's where real beauty and real goodness are.

Patterson: You three have lost me here. The whole aesthetics approach seems to weaken your argument, not strengthen it.

Meyer: Maybe, but I think our point is that there may be some important terms used in art that may be useful again in ethics. Utilitarians and Kantians seem to assume we make decisions in a kind of vacuum with no personal history. Maybe terms like balance, harmony and integrity are relevant today and can add an important dimension to ethical discussions. I don't think we're arguing that ethics is the same as aesthetics but it sure seems more realistic to talk about ethical decisions as part of a continuous life history.

Rice: And it does make some sense psychologically to talk about a well-rounded human character. It seems to be the goal of what good child-raising is all about.

Meyer: The addition of caring to the list of virtues helps to complete the picture, so to speak.

Patterson: I still don't buy the aesthetics tie-in. Anyway, I have a couple students I'm supposed to be meeting soon. I will say I think I have a better understanding of why caring might be useful outside of the family unit itself.

McMillan: I'm also due somewhere else in ten minutes. Unlike John I still have problems with caring and virtue ethics in general but it's been a good discussion. See you all soon.

Meyer: See you Sue. Bye, John. Sharon, I'm having a couple of our mutual friends, Jim Andrews and Elaine Johnson, over for dinner in a couple weeks and I'm wondering if you'd like to join us.

Rice: Yes, I'd be happy to. I haven't seen either one since the conference last year. Let me know the time.

Meyer: Will do. Good seeing you again.

Rice: You too. Bye.

Discussion Questions

1. p. 86: Is it necessary to confront oppressors on their own terms?

2. p. 87: Is it true that our approach to relationships in this society is based on a contract metaphor?

3. pp. 87-88: Do males and females have fundamentally different ways of looking at ethical problems?

4. p. 88: Does it make sense to say that a person can have an "immature" morality?

5. pp. 89-90: Is empathy or caring as important to being human as reason is?

6. pp. 89-90: Are the persecutions and cruelty in human history mainly due to a lack of empathy for each other?

7. p. 90: Should businesses be concerned about promoting empathy for employees?

8. pp. 90-91: Does caring put people to sleep about unjust social structures?

9. pp. 92-93: Is false caring a problem in society? Does it tend to make people cynical?

10. p. 93: Do politicians have any other alternative in a democracy?

11. pp. 95-96: Is there a relationship between good character and beauty?

12. p. 96: When people talk about a person's "real beauty" despite outward appearance, is that just a nice metaphor or is something actual being talked about?

After-Dinner Discussion

Setting: Mary Ann Meyer's home two weeks later. Also present are Jim Andrews, Sharon Rice and Elaine Johnson. After dinner the group retires to Mary Ann's living room. Jim Andrews talks about his speech to the elementary school teachers but then his tone gets much more serious.

Andrews: You know sometimes I wonder about the human race. Did you see where that woman was brutally killed on a bridge in Detroit and people just stood around watching? It makes me doubt whether teaching philosophy, especially ethics, has any effect at all.

Rice: I'm not sure ethics was as important on that bridge as psychology. Studies show that sort of behavior is common when a large group is involved.

Meyer: People pass the buck.

Rice: Right. They think that the other person will do something about it. People spread out responsibility. If you think about it, that's not totally irrational. After all, with a large group you'd think it would be more likely that someone else would do something.

Johnson: As I recall, the thugs may have had weapons too. Interfering with them could have been deadly.

Andrews: Sure, but history also shows times when individuals **have** got involved. I see what you're saying but I don't think psychology is enough to excuse the crowd's behavior. People are just plain cowards too.

Johnson: I don't know, Jim.   Ending up dead yourself doesn't help much.

Andrews: But the woman was being beaten to death!   Some courage might have saved her life.

Meyer: People did call in on their cellular phones. Maybe that was the best they could do.

Andrews: Except that it was pretty clear that by the time the police arrived it would be too late. That was an easy way out. Lack of courage was the main problem.

Rice: What you call courage might seem foolhardy to many people.   Seeing some muscular vicious guy with a weapon might make any act against him look stupid. Most of us are not weight lifters or experts in self-defense.

Meyer: What's the mean on courage in this situation?   Jim, you're claiming the people on the bridge were cowards, Sharon's saying they were reasonable.   What would have been appropriate?

Andrews: Some sort of reasonable action and I do think action was called for. Aristotle says several times that the true test of courage is when a life hangs in the balance. There wasn't any question that an innocent woman's life was in danger and risking your own hide was necessary.

Rice: Easy to say sitting here in a cozy and safe room. Besides, Aristotle didn't know what we know today about the psychology of people in different circumstances.

Johnson: I doubt if all human motivation can be reduced to psychological conditions. I can see what Jim's getting at. Almost any person who's a coward can justify it on some grounds. Part of being a coward is a kind of decision a person makes. We're not passive creatures.

Andrews: Right and it does make sense to talk about a mean for courage in this case. Not just cowardice but rashness was possible on that bridge.

Rice: How? Trying to stop somebody with a weapon when you don't have one sounds rash to me.

Andrews: But that has to be weighed against what was happening in front of their eyes. A woman was being beaten to death. That was a fact. The dangers were potentially real but still only potential dangers. What was happening was actual.

Johnson: I tend to agree with you about cowardice being a factor but I'm not sure where the line was between courage and rashness in this case.

Meyer: Aristotle claims at one point that rash people are overconfident or impetuous. Maybe that's the key.

Andrews: Maybe. The rash person on that bridge would have blindly leaped into the middle of it or would have just assumed without thinking that they could handle it. Their desires wouldn't have had any rational brakes, you might say. But nobody there was rash, that's for sure. Nobody was courageous either. Courage would be thinking before acting but definitely acting.

Rice: Still not sure I buy that. Any action in that case would have been dangerous.

Johnson: To support Jim's point it seems to me something else was involved too. It takes guts to face down danger but there was more than just physical danger involved here. A huge moral violation was occurring right in front of those people. Preventing that violation seems to be the duty of any decent human being.

Meyer: You're right, Elaine.   That's called moral courage in philosophy.

Andrews: It's too bad that poor woman didn't have a moral hero on that bridge.

Meyer: Jim, would you have helped her?

Andrews: Honestly, probably not, and it would have been a major moral failure on my part to watch that woman die while I did nothing.   My own fears would have probably overwhelmed my awareness of what needed to be done.   I would have been a coward and meanwhile an innocent human being dies in front of me.

Rice: I think we all face that sort of moral problem on a smaller scale pretty often.   It's just not usually life or death.   When a friend tells a racist joke, it takes courage to confront the issue.

Johnson: Right.   I see courage in the hospital too, including among the staff.   The way hospital hierarchies are set up, for a nurse or medical technologist to question some physicians takes real courage.   Their job might be on the line.   Their problem is that they're often closer to the patients and can see mistakes.   If they care about the patient and are professionals they've got a duty to question the physician's orders but many are afraid to do that.

Andrews: I don't see physical and moral courage as being very distinct.   The people on the bridge were confronting a moral horror but the danger was physical.   The world doesn't break down neatly into those categories.

Meyer: I'm not saying it does.   All I'm saying is that they are useful categories for thinking about courage.   Physical courage usually involves defending your own physical existence and your loved ones from something threatening. Or it might be facing an enemy in war or saving a child from a burning house. Usually it involves threat of physical pain and possibly death - a basic fear we all have. Moral courage is more about defending moral principles. Elaine's example is excellent. So is Sharon's. In arguing against racist jokes, you're defending a principle and the danger isn't physical pain or death but your reputation and social standing with your friends. It's a different sort of fear we have to face. In Elaine's example it was loss of a job. I wouldn't call those examples physical courage. It's much more a moral issue tied to your life in society.

Rice: I think there might be a third form of courage too. In psychology I see a lot of students trying to cope with personal problems. Many are from homes with an alcoholic parent and some have been abused in some way. I also see students with problems like obsessive-compulsive disorder and phobias. Dealing with those backgrounds and facing those kinds of problems requires courage too.

Meyer: A kind of psychological courage?

Rice: Right. It's not physical courage. Sometimes the students have to confront physical danger but usually not. It's an internal struggle. And I don't think it's moral courage. They're not defending a moral principle as such. Their goal is psychological integrity and to get this they have to confront real pain and fear.

Johnson: I can sure understand your point with alcoholics and drug addicts. Sometimes I have addicted patients being heroic right in front of me. Going to an AA meeting or coming to the hospital for help means facing some strong demons.

Meyer: But can you be courageous against something inside yourself? I mean, I understand your point about facing fear. But in some of the cases you mentioned the fear is based on something imagined. Phobias are based on imaginary dangers.

Andrews: Yeah, I see your point.   Is courage about facing your inner fears or is courage about facing real dangers in the world? For that matter, does fear need to be involved in courage at all? Could you be courageous in a dangerous situation if you had no fear of it?

Rice: You philosophers can make those distinctions if you want. Maybe it's important for clarifying a definition. But I can tell you with no doubt that a 20-year-old who faces the results of abuse and tries to deal with it has my admiration for her courage.   It's a terrifying experience both to admit what happened and then to start out on a new path in life. And I don't know what you'd call it if you don't call it courage.

Meyer: I suppose then cowardice would be giving in to the fear - refusing to face the problem.

Rice: Sure.

Andrews: That seems harsh.   Cowards are people I blame.   I don't blame a phobic for caving in to the anxiety and I don't blame a kid who doesn't want to face an abusive parent.

Meyer: I don't know. We're all cowards to some degree. How often do you or I stand up for a moral principle? Less than we'd like to is my guess. We all want to be accepted. Most people aren't real courageous. I think the people you blame are people who are cowards in important situations - lives on the line, like the bridge example.   But the examples Sharon mentioned are cowards a lot like we are in everyday life. Most of the time we go along with the crowd. Most of the time a phobic gives in to her phobia. Maybe "coward" isn't too strong a term if you think of it that way.

Rice: It's an easier term to accept if you think of an alcoholic or a spouse who is afraid to leave a harmful relationship.

Andrews: Yes. Alcoholics can be destructive to other people's lives. I think "coward" fits there.

Rice: Same with an abusive marriage. Refusing to face up to a destructive marriage might not just affect you; it might affect children also.

Meyer: I can see cowardice but what about rashness in these cases? What would be rashness in an alcoholic?

Johnson: Maybe I've got an example of that. Some people are in the hospital regularly because they kick a drug habit only to go back into it again. They really do want to beat it - they're not cowards - and they're willing to take the risk but they don't do it intelligently. Their desires just swing back and forth like a pendulum without any clear or firm direction.

Rice: Phobics and obsessive - compulsives are often like that too. They'll make an effort to beat the problem but they sometimes do it without much guidance and help. They're afraid sometimes to admit they need help. People try to be loners. A claustrophobic may just do the avoided behavior out of sheer will power but that often just reinforces the fear.

Andrews: So, if running away from the fear is being cowardly and facing it blindly is being rash, what's the mean? How do you use reason to guide desires in a case like this?

Rice: Face the problem but do it reflectively, I'd say. Usually that means getting help from other people and that can be tough on a person's self-image. A lot of people have problems they want to face but don't want to look bad or have their self-image damaged so they won't ask for help. They just launch off and attack the problem on their own with no guidance. That would be rashness if I understand Mary Ann right.

Meyer: Vanity and self-image have a lot to do with rashness. Aristotle talks about rash military people who want to look good so they do stupid things to look brave.

Andrews: I like your point, Sharon, about using reason to get help and I was thinking of Elaine's example of the alcoholic. Wouldn't temperance be a more important virtue here? When I think of breaking bad habits, I think of acting on the appropriate level of desire - eating, drinking, whatever. Not sure courage is that important.

Rice: Maybe it depends on the habit.

Johnson: Right. I think it has to do with the level of dependency. I definitely see courage in facing alcoholism or a drug habit. I don't see it in my attempt to break my habit of eating too many snack foods. There's a lot of pain to face in breaking a drug habit.

Rice: And a bigger fear about facing the future without the habit. Drug addicts are terrified of a future without the drug.

Meyer: I even think a little courage might be involved in breaking the snack habit. There's always some anxiety about changing any lifestyle - something about an unknown future. Maybe in major bad habits courage is most important and temperance less so. In minor bad habits temperance is more important and courage much less so.

Rice: Temperance might be an issue when it comes to bad habits and addictions but I don't think it's an issue at all for students who come from abusive homes. They have no current pleasure, just a scary unknown future.

Same with spousal abuse. Courage is everything. It's not a matter of giving in to pleasures.

Johnson: I don't know. Some people in abusive marriages do get something out of it. There's a kind of security that they sometimes don't want to give up. My colleagues in psychiatry claim women in abusive marriages often don't think very highly of themselves and think the marriage they're in is the best they can do in life. It's a sort of security blanket for a weak self-image.

Rice: I'm not sure I'd call hanging onto a security blanket a lack of temperance. It's a fear of giving it up that motivates them. Courage is the main issue.

Meyer: I keep wondering where patience comes into this. No relationship is perfect - all of them have tough times to work through. Spousal abuse is clearly wrong but a lot of marriages are mixed bags - they've got some good points and some negative ones. Patience is a virtue too. It's not one Aristotle talks about but some modern virtue theorists do. It's putting your desires on hold, so to speak.

Johnson: A patient person expects a situation to get better. Maybe that's the key. If a marriage partner can really expect a situation to improve, then he or she should be patient, otherwise have the courage to change.

Andrews: But in some marriages a spouse may know it'll never improve but still have reasons for keeping the marriage going. I don't think patience has to necessarily involve a better future. It might involve a situation where a person thinks the good outweighs the bad so they put up with the bad. I suspect that's pretty common in marriages.

Meyer: In both cases patience could be a front for cowardice. I have a friend who's always talking about patient love because she thinks her husband will change his bad habits. But he hasn't changed in twelve years so he probably won't now. I think she's really afraid to act but she says she's patient so she can avoid the truth and avoid acting.

Johnson: I'm not sure you can draw a clear line between real and false patience. Some people really are more patient.

Rice: But Mary Ann has a good point. Some of what passes for patience is self-deception. A person convinces herself that the situation is just great despite overwhelming negative evidence. We deceive ourselves a lot and false patience is one way.

Johnson: Some people have a kind of self-deceptive patience when they're terminally ill. They don't want to face the truth and think they are just waiting to get better. It's a form of denial.

Andrews: But is that a vice? From what I understand it's a stage many terminally ill patients go through. Maybe it's necessary and healthy for them at the time.

Johnson: I don't think denial is good. Maybe it's necessary at times but that doesn't make it a positive trait. I deal with patients who stay in denial for long periods of time. They never come to grips with their disease and can never deal with their families or reality, for that matter. When their family comes to see them, sometimes the family supports the deception and then nobody ever really expresses how they feel about the truth of the matter. It's sad. When the family tries to break through the denial, they feel they aren't expressing love for the patient and sometimes the patient implies that to them. Denial may be necessary in some people but I think it's a really negative mind set.

Rice: I think it's a vice too. A huge number of psychological problems depend on self-deception.

Andrews: I don't know. I'm more of a utilitarian on self-deception. It's something I talk about in my ethics course. It seems to me that it depends completely on the situation. I mean I remember falling in love and thinking the other person was the greatest human being on the planet. Evidence didn't indicate that but who cares about evidence when you're in love. I was deceiving myself at least part of the time but I wouldn't want to give up the experience. It's part of being human.

Rice: Did you marry that person?

Andrews: No.

Rice: Probably good. People who marry from infatuation often are sorry.

Meyer: That might indicate your self-deception wasn't that harmless.

Andrews: A marriage based on it might be bad. But the high of infatuation is itself good. Nobody would ever have the experience if we all went around being super-objective about other people.

Meyer: I'd still argue self-deception is a negative character trait but it's a trait that can get overwhelmed at times by other positive factors. Jim, face it, if you kept deceiving yourself about that person, your life decisions would be based on illusions. Sharon's right. If you married the person based on self-deception, you might end up in a marriage like the one we were discussing before - lots of kidding yourself about the relationship. I'll grant you falling in love is great but it's temporary and the emotional high overwhelms the negative factors. But based on that I don't think we want to argue self-deception should become a habit. It's a bad habit.

Andrews: But why should truth be the number one concern all the time? All this talk about the good of being honest with yourself assumes there's only one value in life - truth. Why can't emotions or artistic expression be just as important? If they are, then maybe self-deception is OK at times.

Rice: It's funny but I guess I think of truth differently than you do. In psychology we assume that someone who admits a fear to herself admits a truth. Why aren't emotions truths?

Meyer: Good point, Sharon. I hadn't looked at it that way. Maybe we're assuming that truth just means objective evidence so a person who falls in love is somehow putting emotion against truth. But the feeling of infatuation is a truth itself for the person. So maybe the conflict isn't between emotion and truth but between two kinds of truth. Does that make any sense?

Andrews: I don't know. I remember reading an article once about self-deception in which the author claimed that deceiving yourself can actually be a positive sign of love. I think the example he used was a mother deceiving herself about her severely injured son. It was a sign of her deep love that she refused to believe he might die. That seems right to me. Self-deception showed the depth of her love.

Meyer: I'm not clear why self-deception was necessary in that case. If Sharon's right then the conflict wasn't between the emotion of love and the truth about her son. It was between the truth of her love for her son and the truth about her son's condition - a conflict of truths. Why does self-deception about her son's health show more love?

Johnson: Right. Sometimes in the emergency room a man will deceive himself about his wife's condition but I've also observed many spouses who don't deceive themselves and weep openly about the situation. It's sure not clear to me that self-deception somehow shows greater love. I think it has more to do with wanting to hang on to someone you need rather than love for the person herself. In fact I might even say that self-deception in that case is **less** loving because instead of recognizing the truth about the injured person you're more concerned about yourself.

Andrews: I'll grant you that case but I don't think that fits the infatuation case. Even if I admit that the feeling of infatuation is a type of truth, my argument is that the truth of that feeling justifies deceiving yourself about the truth of the other person at times.

Rice: I see Jim's point but here's another example that impresses me more. Sometimes psychologists joke about "artistic neurosis." A lot of great artists in history had terrible lives as children. They were often well off physically but their psychological upbringing was terrible. An adult artist has only so much time and energy. I've heard it said by some psychologists that if certain artists ever tried to cure the problems they had, they would have no time or energy left for art. In fact, they might not be very good artists if they did cure their problems since art can be an outlet for feelings. So maybe their artistic ability makes it worth deceiving themselves about the truth of their childhood. In that case self-deception might be a positive good and even a good habit for those people.

Meyer: Why do they have to deceive themselves about it? Why can't they just admit the problem is there and just go on with their work?

Rice: I'm sure that happens. But I'll bet it also happens for some people that kidding themselves about their problems is what makes their creativity possible. That's certainly a possible scenario and in that case self-deception might be a valuable good.

Johnson: Do you really believe that?

Rice: As a psychologist I think it's best if people admit and
               work on personal problems to improve their lives. I
               guess I just think there may be exceptions.

Meyer: But I don't think the exception destroys my point.
               Honesty with other people may be a virtue but
               that doesn't mean it can always be applied. I would lie
               to save an innocent life. Same with self-honesty.

Andrews: So you're admitting that self-deception might be a good
               habit in certain people.

Meyer: I'm saying there may be situations in which it may be
               necessary. That doesn't make it a good habit any more
               than having to lie at times makes lying a good habit. I
               mean think of living in some tyrannical society - under
               Stalin say. The slightest hint of independent thought
               may get you and your family killed. So you learn very
               young to lie and maybe deceive yourself and it becomes
               a way to survive. But that doesn't make it an
               intrinsically good trait! Without those very special
               circumstances it's a harmful trait. That might be the
               case with the artist too. Self-deception as a habit is
               still a vice but it may in some cases be a necessary vice.

Johnson: As a philosophical outsider it seems to me you both
               have a point. Self-deception may have been useful
               under Stalin but self-honesty's a virtue because it's
               proven itself good in the long run. Self-deception
               hasn't. If I deceived my patients and myself as a
               physician, both my patients and I would be in big
               trouble. So I agree that self-honesty's a virtue.

Rice: I've always thought of self-deception like lying to a
               friend except the friend is yourself. You almost owe
               yourself honesty the way you owe it to a friend.

Meyer: Sure. Aristotle said something similar. You have to care about yourself before you can care about someone else. If you're not honest with yourself first, you'll develop a habit that will make it impossible to be honest with a friend. You'll never have complete friends then.

Johnson: Are complete friends people you never would lie to? Not sure I have any of those - no offense to present company.

Andrews: Complete friends are what we might call true friends or best friends. It's a term from Aristotle.

Johnson: So there are complete friends and incomplete friends?

Andrews: Actually Aristotle says there are three kinds. Friends for usefulness are one group. Friends for pleasure are another one. Complete friends are the third.

Johnson: I guess I don't see what makes a complete friend different. Don't you enjoy being with them? Don't you do things for one another? Aren't all friends for usefulness or pleasure?

Meyer: Based on what we were talking about just now I guess Aristotle might say that you'd be willing to lie to friends for usefulness or pleasure at times but you really wouldn't hold anything back from a complete friend.

Rice: But why would you lie to any of them? We've already established that honesty is a virtue.

Meyer: Think of friends you have who are friends because you work together. That's an example of what Aristotle means by friends for utility or usefulness. You might not tell the whole truth to them about your home life because you think that's not their concern and you might have a point. Or take somebody you enjoy socializing with but not much else. That would be a friend for pleasure. You might fudge things with them when it came to what's happening at work because what happens at work is not everyone's business. You don't make a habit of lying to people but not everything about you is another person's business. The trick is to deal with that without making lying a way of life.

Rice: Really superficial friends then.

Meyer: Aristotle would agree they're superficial but that doesn't make such friendships evil or harmful - just shallow. It's great to have friends for utility or pleasure.

Andrews: So you're saying lying is OK to them if the topic is none of their business?

Meyer: No. Lying is still a bad habit to get into and Kant would say they still deserve the truth. But there's also such a thing as preserving the privacy of other people - your spouse, the people you work with. If somebody is asking about those areas, you have a duty to those other people to protect their rights.

Johnson: I'm still vague on this complete friend idea. So you would never lie to a complete friend?

Meyer: Frankly, no, you wouldn't. Aristotle says a complete friend is like another self. Each helps the other flourish in life. They're people you should be able to share anything with - complete trust.

Rice: Isn't that what marriage is supposed to be?

Meyer: Ideally. Despite his outdated and wrong views about women, Aristotle says the ideal marriage is when the two spouses are complete friends. That's a great point. When we discuss it in class I've had some students tell me that their complete friend is not their spouse but someone else.

Johnson: So in that case you might lie to your spouse before you'd lie to your friend?

Meyer: Yes. A just and honest person wouldn't lie to either but the motivation might be different in each case. One is out of duty, the other out of friendship. Aristotle has this beautiful line when he says that if people are friends they don't need justice but just people need friends in addition. You would not lie to a complete friend. It's in the nature of the friendship. Justice is included in complete friendship, you might say. But the just person who doesn't lie to anyone on principle still is lacking something without friends.

Johnson: But I want to get this straight. You could more easily lie to a spouse who wasn't a complete friend than to some third party who was one. Right?

Meyer: Yes, if justice demanded such a lie.

Andrews: I suppose that might happen if some private point about the complete friend came up in the marriage. You'd protect that person's privacy by lying to your spouse.

Rice: But then the opposite would **not** hold. If you're totally honest with a complete friend, what about your spouse's privacy? I don't think I like that scenario at all.

Johnson: Neither do I. It sounds like a great reason why spouses should be best friends with each other. Lots of potential conflicts otherwise.

Meyer: Yes but a complete friend would understand your dilemma. A complete friend wouldn't ask about your spouse because he or she would know you would be forced to violate your spouse's privacy. If your friend did ask, it might be a sign that he or she was more interested in gossip or juicy information than in your welfare. The person might not be a complete friend.

Rice: You're assuming a complete friend is some sort of saint. People slip at times.

Meyer: Sure. That's why Aristotle says complete friendship is possible only between virtuous people. They slip less and can care about somebody besides themselves. I think virtuous people also understand that nobody's perfect so they might be more forgiving too.

Johnson: So Aristotle is saying bad people can't be complete friends?

Meyer: Right.

Johnson: But there are plenty of cases where criminals are close friends.

Andrews: Usefulness.

Meyer: Yes. They might be friends until their own selfishness got in the way. All Aristotle is saying is really common sense. People who develop selfish habits simply will have a much more difficult time empathizing with a friend. And even if they can, their selfishness will be like a boundary in the friendship. Two jewel thieves might be friends until one of them wants to become an open and just person. Since that threatens the lifestyle of the first, the friendship would end.

Andrews: I see your point, Mary Ann, but how is that different from two good people who are friends and one of them changes for the worse? Wouldn't that cramp the style of the virtuous one? Sounds like the same reasoning to me.

Meyer: One big difference. Complete friends who are good people care about each other's flourishing. If your complete friend turns to drugs, you would do your best to help him. If the friendship breaks off it would be because you simply have become too different to be friends. It's sad. But a vicious person's focus is on himself. If his buddy turns virtuous on him it threatens his personal interest. That's why the friendship ends.

Johnson: Still not sure I agree that bad people can't be complete friends. They have one corner of their life where they can have complete trust. If both people agree that they won't touch other areas of their lives, they could be complete friends.

Rice: Pretty shaky friendship. The smaller the corner of their life, the less they can talk about and share. It would seem those other areas are important. If you don't share much, the friendship doesn't seem complete.

Meyer: Those are the boundaries between them I mentioned earlier. Aristotle says the vicious person's soul is in conflict. Desires clash in the person. Vicious people can have plenty of friends for utility or pleasure but I think Aristotle was right that complete friendship depends on decent character on both sides. It's probably a matter of degree. The better the human beings involved, the deeper the friendship can be.

Johnson: You talked about mutual welfare of friends. But if you're expecting something from your friend, isn't that selfish? There's a usefulness factor in all friendship.

Meyer: Aristotle says something about that which always strikes me as true. He says the true joy of friendship is in loving not in being loved.

Andrews: I think Aristotle is right but if you never got anything in return the loving part would be tough to continue. You need something for yourself.

Meyer: But you don't relate to a true friend looking for that, at least usually. Aristotle's point is that your focus should be on the good of the other person. That's the real joy of sharing. Even with friends for utility or pleasure, I think the best part is the sharing aspect. You help each other on a project or you share a good time together. Your active role is critical. With complete friends you can forget about yourself the most. If you were worried about what you were going to get out of it, the friendship wouldn't be very enjoyable.

Johnson: Sounds kind of mystical. I know what my interests are. All this giving stuff sounds so vague. I don't really know what **your** interests are and, besides, why should I put them first? Does Aristotle give any reasons?

Meyer: He claims mutual sharing creates the strongest friendships that last the longest. But when you come down to it I think he's appealing to our experience. It's not a logical argument. It's a kind of experience. Sharing is richer than taking and sharing with a friend is a deep part of human happiness.

Rice: I think with a friend happiness comes from giving of your skill as a human being, so to speak - using your mind to care about somebody else.

Meyer: Aristotle would put it as using your mind to guide your desires toward someone else's good.

Johnson: It's what we call good will today.

Meyer: Not really. I can have good will toward somebody and she wouldn't be a friend.

Rice: Mutual good will then.

Meyer: You and the clerk at the convenience store can have mutual good will toward each other and you aren't friends either. Aristotle claims friendship is mutual good will that is recognized by both parties involved. Closer but not enough, I think. The clerk and I can recognize and appreciate that we have good will toward each other and not be friends.

Johnson: So what's the missing ingredient?

Meyer: Acting for each other's good. Mutual good will might be the beginning of a friendship - a shared attitude toward each other that you each recognize. But real friendship involves acting for each other and sharing emotions, not just having a certain attitude. Maybe that's what Aristotle meant; he talks a lot about sharing time together. Mutual good will as an attitude is too weak to be called friendship.

Johnson: Assuming that there are complete friends like you've argued, how many of these can you have?

Meyer: Not many if Aristotle is right.

Rice: I would guess very few - one or two at most. The time and energy put into friendships like that would make it impossible to have more.

Meyer: That's what Aristotle says too. It takes too much time to have more than one or two. But I had an older student a couple semesters ago who said she had about a dozen complete friends.

Andrews: How could anybody manage that? Maybe she had friends for utility and pleasure mixed up with complete friends.

Meyer: She claimed she could maintain contact by telephone so she didn't have to spend physical time with her friends. She said she even kept contact by phone with a complete friend on the other side of the country.

Johnson: Interesting. Maybe in Aristotle's day it was impossible to have more than one or two complete friends because you had to be physically with them to talk. But now with phones and e-mail we don't have to be there physically so we can have more. I never thought of technology's effect on friendship.

Andrews: I'm not sure people you call once in a while can be complete friends.

Meyer: My student claimed that they had developed a close trusting relationship earlier in life and that was still there. She says they didn't call each other just because the caller needed help. They called each other to maintain the relationship and share each other's lives.

Rice: I'm not sure I'd accept that claim at face value. Part of friendship is body language, small emotional expressions, things you can only experience while you're physically with the other person. I can see how a phone call or e-mail could maintain a close relationship but I really think something is lost if the person's not there, especially for any length of time. I think it's impossible to maintain the same level of friendship over long distance because you would lose those small clues about the other person's life.

Andrews: Something else too. Part of being a friend is growing together over time. If you don't see somebody for years, phone calls can never make up for the time shared together. Phone calls or e-mail messages might be like snapshots of the person's life at the time but not the actual life.

Rice: And if you call someone once a month or whatever, that month between calls is a long time in which you haven't helped the other person grow and develop. The point of being together a lot is not just enjoyment but to help one another become better human beings. That takes actual time spent together.

Johnson: I'm afraid it's getting late. I have to be going. But, speaking of friends, I have to admit I feel a sense of trust in this group. We've been able to disagree and still respect each other and we've been able to open up with each other more than I do with my colleagues at the hospital. I wonder how we would describe our friendship. Do complete friends talk about being complete friends?

Meyer: Why not? Complete friendship often begins with being friends for pleasure. It was sure a good start tonight.

Andrews: I have to be heading out too.   Maybe complete friendship is a matter of degree, not a cut and dried distinction. I share Elaine's feelings. Thanks for the marvelous evening, Mary Ann.

Rice: Yes. Thank you for inviting me. I'll probably see you around campus in the next couple days.

Meyer: Thank you all for coming. Good night.

Discussion Questions

1. p. 100:   Does the psychology of crowd behavior justify inaction in cases like this?

2. pp. 100-1:   Is being a coward a decision a person makes?

3. p. 101:   What would be courage in this situation?

4. p. 102:   Does Andrews weaken his argument by his own admission here?

5. p. 103:   Is there such a thing as "psychological courage?"

6. p. 104:   Respond to the questions Andrews raises about courage.

7. p. 104:   Would the term "coward" fit someone giving in to a phobia?

8. pp. 105-6:   Is vanity the major reason people will not seek help when they need it?

9. p. 106:   Is courage involved at all in breaking minor bad habits like the "snack habit?"

10. p. 108:   Is denial good? Why or why not?

11. pp. 108-9:   Is infatuation a form of self-deception?

12. p. 109:   Are there elements of life besides truth which are just as important as truth and which would justify self-deception?

13. pp. 110-11:   Is self-deception over a dying loved one a sign of love or selfishness?

14. p. 111:   Is the artist example a positive form of self-deception?

15. pp. 111-12: Is self-deception intrinsically harmful in some way or is it always a utilitarian question?

16. pp. 113-14: Are there complete friends? Is Aristotle's distinction between types of friends accurate?

17. pp. 114-15: Could you live with the situation in a marriage in which you and your spouse were not complete friends?

18. pp. 114-15: Could you live with the situation in a marriage in which your spouse had a complete friend other than you? Under what conditions?

19. pp. 116-17: Can criminals be complete friends?

20. pp. 117-18: Should complete friends be willing to share **everything**?

21. p. 119: How many complete friends can a person have?

22. pp. 119-20: Can you maintain complete friendship by telephone or e-mail?

23. pp. 119-20: How far can friendship develop from the beginning by e-mail or chat rooms?

Further Reading

Part I

Thursday

Aristotle's concept of virtue: Virtue and cultural relativism

Aristotle. *Nicomachean Ethics*. Translated by Terence Irwin. Indianapolis: Hackett, 1985.

Aronson, Elliot. *The Social Animal*. 4th ed. New York: Freeman, 1984.

Barnes, Jonathan. *Aristotle*. New York: Oxford University Press, 1982.

Benedict, Ruth. *Patterns of Culture*. Boston: Houghton Mifflin, 1989.

Guthrie, W.K.C. *The Greek Philosophers: From Thales to Aristotle*. New York: Harper & Row, 1975.

Kohlberg, Lawrence. *The Philosophy of Moral Development*. San Francisco: Harper & Row, 1981.

Maslow, Abraham. *Motivation and Personality*. 3rd ed. New York: Harpercollins, 1987.

Midgley, Mary. *Beast and Man: The Roots of Human Nature*. Revised ed. London: Routledge, 1995.

Plato. *Republic*. Translated by Desmond Lee. London: Penguin, 1987.

Plato. *The Last Days of Socrates*. Translated by Hugh Tredennick and Harold Tarrant. London: Penguin, 1993.

Robinson, Timothy A. *Aristotle in Outline*. Indianapolis: Hackett, 1995.

Sabini, John and **Maury Silver**. *Moralities of Everyday Life*. New York: Oxford University Press, 1982.

Service, Elman. *Profiles in Ethnology*. 3rd ed. New York: Harpercollins, 1990.

Turnbull, Colin. *The Mountain People*. New York: Touchstone Books, 1987.

Wilson, James Q. *The Moral Sense*. New York: The Free Press, 1993.

Friday

Virtue and egoism; Virtue and utilitarianism

Bentham, Jeremy. *The Principles of Morals and Legislation.* New York: Free Press, 1970.

Deci, Edward. Effects of Externally Mediated Rewards on Intrinsic Motivation. *Journal of Personality and Social Psychology.* Vol. 18 (1971): 103-115.

Foot, Philippa. *Virtues and Vices and Other Essays in Moral Philosophy.* Berkeley: University of California Press, 1979.

Lepper, Mark and **David Greene**. Undermining Children's Intrinsic Interest with Extrinsic Reward. *Journal of Personality and Social Psychology.* Vol. 28 (1973): 129-137.

MacIntyre, Alasdair. *After Virtue.* 2nd ed. Notre Dame: University of Notre Dame Press, 1984.

Mill, J.S. *On Liberty.* Edited by Currin Shields. Indianapolis: Bobbs-Merrill, 1956.

Mill, J.S.. *Utilitarianism.* Edited by Oskar Piest. Indianapolis: Bobbs-Merrill, 1976.

Pincoffs, Edmund L. *Quandaries and Virtues: Against Reductivism in Ethics.* Lawrence, KS: University Press of Kansas, 1986.

Putman, Daniel. Egoism and Virtue. *Journal of Value Inquiry.* Vol. 26 (1992): 117-124.

Slote, Michael. *Goods and Virtues.* Oxford: Clarendon Press, 1990.

White, Robert W. Motivation Reconsidered: The Concept of Competence. *Psychological Review.* Vol. 66 (1959): 297-333.

Saturday

Virtue and rights; Virtue and medicine

Beauchamp, Tom and **James Childress**. *Principles of Biomedical Ethics*. 4th ed. New York: Oxford University Press, 1994.

Bok, Sissela. *Lying: Moral Choice in Public and Private Life*. New York: Vintage, 1989.

Brody, Howard. *Ethical Decisions in Medicine*. 2nd ed. Boston: Little Brown, 1981.

Engelhardt, Jr., H. Tristram. *The Foundations of Bioethics*. New York: Oxford University Press, 1996.

Gewirth, Alan. *Reason and Morality*. Chicago: University of Chicago Press, 1982.

Kant, Immanuel. *Groundwork of the Metaphysics of Morals*. Translated by H.J. Paton. New York: Harper & Row, 1964.

Lombardi, Louis. *Moral Analysis: Foundations, Guides and Applications*. Albany: SUNY Press, 1988.

Mappes, Thomas and **David DeGrazia** (eds.). *Biomedical Ethics*, 4th ed. New York: McGraw-Hill, 1996.

Putman, Daniel. Rights and Virtues: Toward an Integrated Theory. *Journal of Value Inquiry*. Vol. 21 (1987): 87-99.

Putman, Daniel. Virtue and the Practice of Modern Medicine. *Journal of Medicine and Philosophy*. Vol. 13 (1988): 433-43.

Regan, Tom. *The Case for Animal Rights*. Berkeley: University of California Press, 1985.

Shelp, E.E. (ed.). *Virtue and Medicine*. Dordrecht, Holland: D. Reidel, 1985.

Veatch, Robert. The Danger of Virtue. *Journal of Medicine and Philosophy*. Vol. 13 (1988): 445-46.

128 Human Excellence

Part II

Awards Ceremony

Virtue and honor; Virtue and children

Baumrind, Diana. The Development of Instrumental Competence through Socialization. In A.D. Pick (ed.). *Minnesota Symposium on Child Psychology*. Vol. 7. Minneapolis: University of Minnesota Press, 1973.

Cordner, Christopher. Aristotelian Virtue and Its Limitations. *Philosophy*. Vol. 69 (1994): 291-316.

Damon, William. *The Moral Child: Nurturing Children's Natural Moral Growth*. New York: The Free Press, 1990.

Damon, William. *Greater Expectations: Overcoming the Culture of Indulgence in Our Homes and Schools*. New York: Free Press, 1996.

Maccoby, Eleanore. *Social Development: Psychological Growth and the Parent-Child Relationship*. New York: Harcourt Brace Jovanovich, 1980.

Piaget, Jean. *The Moral Judgment of the Child*. New York: The Free Press, 1997.

Putman, Daniel. In Defence of Aristotelian Honour. *Philosophy*. Vol. 70 (1995): 286-288.

Putman, Daniel. The Primacy of Virtue in Children's Moral Development. *Journal of Moral Education*. Vol. 24 (1995): 175-183.

Conference on Feminism and Ethics

Virtue and the ethics of care; Virtue and aesthetics

Baier, Annette. Trust and Antitrust. *Ethics*. Vol. 96 (1986): 231-260.

English, Jane (ed.). *Sex Equality*. Englewood Cliffs, NJ: Prentice-Hall, 1977.

Gilligan, Carol. *In a Different Voice*. Cambridge: Harvard, 1982.

Mahowald, Mary (ed.). *Philosophy of Woman: An Anthology of Classic to Current Concepts*. 3rd ed. Indianapolis: Hackett, 1994.

Mill, J.S. *The Subjection of Women*. Edited by Susan Okin. Indianapolis: Hackett, 1988.

Noddings, Nell. *Caring: A Feminine Approach to Ethics and Moral Education*. Berkeley: University of California Press, 1986.

Plato. *Symposium*. Translated by Walter Hamilton. London: Penguin, 1995.

Putman, Daniel. Relational Ethics and Virtue Theory. *Metaphilosophy*. Vol. 22 (1991): 231-238.

Sabini, John and **Maury Silver**. Character: The Moral and the Aesthetic. *International Journal of Moral and Social Studies*. Vol. 2 (1987): 189-200.

Tong, Rosemarie. *Feminine and Feminist Ethics*. Belmont, CA: Wadsworth, 1993.

Wallace, James. *Virtues and Vices*. Ithaca, NY: Cornell University Press, 1978.

After-Dinner Discussion

Nature of courage; Virtue and self-deception; Virtue and friendship

Callann, Eamonn. Patience and Courage. *Philosophy*. Vol. 68 (1993): 523-539.

Fingarette, Herbert. *Self-Deception*. London: Routledge, 1969.

Lockard, Joan and **Delroy Paulhus** (eds.). *Self-Deception: An Adaptive Mechanism?* Englewood Cliffs, NJ: Prentice-Hall, 1988.

Martin, Mike W. *Self-Deception and Morality*. Lawrence, KS: University Press of Kansas, 1988.

Martin Mike (ed.). *Self-Deception and Self-Understanding*. Lawrence, KS: University Press of Kansas, 1985.

Mele, Alfred. *Irrationality: An Essay in Akrasia, Self-Deception and Self-Control*. New York: Oxford University Press, 1987.

Putman, Daniel. Psychological Courage. *Philosophy, Psychiatry and Psychology*. Vol. 4 (1997): 1-11.

Putman, Daniel. Virtue and Self-Deception. *The Southern Journal of Philosophy*. Vol. 25(1987): 549-557.

Stern-Gillet, Suzanne. *Aristotle's Philosophy of Friendship*. Albany: SUNY Press, 1995.

Szabados, Bela. The Morality of Self-Deception. *Dialogue*. Vol. 13 (1974): 25-34.

Thomas, Laurence. *Living Morally: A Psychology of Moral Character*. Philadelphia: Temple University Press, 1989.

Walton, Douglas. *Courage: A Philosophical Investigation*. Berkeley: University of California Press, 1986.

INDEX

The terms "virtue" and "character" occur throughout the book and are not listed in the Index.

About the Author

Daniel Putman is Professor of Philosophy at the University of Wisconsin - Fox Valley. He is the author of over 25 articles on ethics and virtue theory in professional journals such as *Philosophy*, *Journal of Social Philosophy*, *American Philosophical Quarterly*, *Teaching Philosophy*, *Journal of Value Inquiry*, *Journal of Moral Education* and *Philosophy, Psychiatry and Psychology* .